# At the Sign of the Jack O'Lantern

## Myrtle Reed

### [ZHINGOORA BOOKS]

This edition is published by
Zhingoora Books.

# Contents

# I

## The End of the Honeymoon

It was certainly a queer house. Even through the blinding storm they could distinguish its eccentric outlines as they alighted from the stage. Dorothy laughed happily, heedless of the fact that her husband's umbrella was dripping down her neck. "It's a dear old place," she cried; "I love it already!"

For an instant a flash of lightning turned the peculiar windows into sheets of flame, then all was dark again. Harlan's answer was drowned by a crash of thunder and the turning of the heavy wheels on the gravelled road.

"Don't stop," shouted the driver; "I'll come up to-morrer for the money. Good luck to you—an' the Jack-o'-Lantern!"

"What did he mean?" asked Dorothy, shaking out her wet skirts, when they were safely inside the door. "Who's got a Jack-o'-Lantern?"

"You can search me," answered Harlan, concisely, fumbling for a match. "I suppose we've got it. Anyhow, we'll have a look at this sepulchral mansion presently."

His deep voice echoed and re-echoed through the empty rooms, and Dorothy laughed; a little hysterically this time. Match after match sputtered and failed. "Couldn't have got much wetter if I'd been in swimming," he grumbled. "Here goes the last one."

By the uncertain light they found a candle and Harlan drew a long breath of relief. "It would have been pleasant, wouldn't it?" he went on. "We could have sat on the stairs until morning, or broken our admirable necks in falling over strange furniture. The next thing is a fire. Wonder where my distinguished relative kept his wood?"

Lighting another candle, he went off on a tour of investigation, leaving Dorothy alone.

She could not repress a shiver as she glanced around the gloomy room. The bare loneliness of the place was accentuated by the depressing furniture, which belonged to the black walnut and haircloth period. On the marble-topped table, in the exact centre of the room, was a red plush album, flanked on one side by a hideous china vase, and on the other by a basket of wax flowers under a glass shade.

Her home-coming! How often she had dreamed of it, never for a moment guessing that it might be like this! She had fancied a little house in a suburb, or a cosy apartment in the city, and a lump came into her throat as her air castle dissolved into utter ruin. She was one of those rare, unhappy women whose natures are so finely attuned to beauty that ugliness hurts like physical pain.

She sat down on one of the slippery haircloth chairs, facing the mantel where the single candle threw its tiny light afar. Little by little the room crept into shadowy relief—the melodeon in the corner, the what-not, with its burden of incongruous ornaments, and even the easel bearing the crayon portrait of the former mistress of the house, becoming faintly visible.

Presently, from above the mantel, appeared eyes. Dorothy felt them first, then looked up affrighted. From the darkness they gleamed upon her in a way that made her heart stand still. Human undoubtedly, but not in the least friendly, they were the eyes of one who bitterly resented the presence of an intruder. The light flickered, then flamed up once more and brought into view the features that belonged with the eyes.

Dorothy would have screamed, had it not been for the lump in her throat. A step came nearer and nearer, from some distant part of the house, accompanied by a cheery, familiar whistle. Still the stern, malicious face held her spellbound, and even when Harlan came in with his load of wood, she could not turn away.

"Now," he said, "we'll start a fire and hang ourselves up to dry."

"What is it?" asked Dorothy, her lips scarcely moving.

His eyes followed hers. "Uncle Ebeneezer's portrait," he answered. "Why, Dorothy Carr! I believe you're scared!"

"I was scared," she admitted, reluctantly, after a brief silence, smiling a little at her own foolishness. "It's so dark and gloomy in here, and you were gone so long——"

Her voice trailed off into an indistinct murmur, but she still shuddered in spite of herself.

"Funny old place," commented Harlan, kneeling on the hearth and laying kindlings, log-cabin fashion, in the fireplace. "If an architect planned it, he must have gone crazy the week before he did it."

"Or at the time. Don't, dear—wait a minute. Let's light our first fire together."

He smiled as she slipped to her knees beside him, and his hand held hers while the blazing splinter set the pine kindling aflame. Quickly the whole room was aglow with light and warmth, in cheerful contrast to the stormy tumult outside.

"Somebody said once," observed Harlan, as they drew their chairs close to the hearth, "that four feet on a fender are sufficient for happiness."

"Depends altogether on the feet," rejoined Dorothy, quickly. "I wouldn't want Uncle Ebeneezer sitting here beside me—no disrespect intended to your relation, as such."

"Poor old duck," said Harlan, kindly. "Life was never very good to him, and Death took away the only thing he ever loved.

"Aunt Rebecca," he continued, feeling her unspoken question. "She died suddenly, when they had been married only three or four weeks."

"Like us," whispered Dorothy, for the first time conscious of a tenderness toward the departed Mr. Judson, of Judson Centre.

"It was four weeks ago to-day, wasn't it?" he mused, instinctively seeking her hand.

"I thought you'd forgotten," she smiled back at him. "I feel like an old married woman, already."

"You don't look it," he returned, gently. Few would have called her beautiful, but love brings beauty with it, and Harlan saw an exquisite loveliness in the deep, dark eyes, the brown hair that rippled and shone in the firelight, the smooth, creamy skin, and the sensitive mouth that betrayed every passing mood.

"None the less, I am," she went on. "I've grown so used to seeing 'Mrs. James Harlan Carr' on my visiting cards that I've forgotten there ever was such a person as 'Miss Dorothy Locke,' who used to get letters, and go calling when she wasn't too busy, and have things sent to her when she had the money to buy them."

"I hope—" Harlan stumbled awkwardly over the words—"I hope you'll never be sorry."

"I haven't been yet," she laughed, "and it's four whole weeks. Come, let's go on an exploring expedition. I'm dry both inside and out, and most terribly hungry."

Each took a candle and Harlan led the way, in and out of unexpected doors, queer, winding passages, and lonely, untenanted rooms. Originally, the house had been simple enough in structure, but wing after wing had been added until the first design, if it could be dignified by that name, had been wholly obscured. From each room branched a series of apartments—a sitting-room, surrounded by bedrooms, each of which contained two or sometimes three beds. A combined kitchen and dining-room was in every separate wing, with an outside door.

"I wonder," cried Dorothy, "if we've come to an orphan asylum!"

"Heaven knows what we've come to," muttered Harlan. "You know I never was here before."

"Did Uncle Ebeneezer have a large family?"

"Only Aunt Rebecca, who died very soon, as I told you. Mother was his only sister, and I her only child, so it wasn't on our side."

"Perhaps," observed Dorothy, "Aunt Rebecca had relations."

"One, two, three, four, five," counted Harlan. "There are five sets of apartments on this side, and three on the other. Let's go upstairs."

From the low front door a series of low windows extended across the house on each side, abundantly lighting the two front rooms, which were separated by the wide hall. A high, narrow window in the lower hall, seemingly with no purpose whatever, began far above the low door and ended abruptly at the ceiling. In the upper hall, a similar window began at the floor and extended upward no higher than Harlan's knees. As Dorothy said, "one would have to lie down to look out of it," but it lighted the hall, which, after all, was the main thing.

In each of the two front rooms, upstairs, was a single round window, too high for one to look out of without standing on a chair, though in both rooms there was plenty of side light. One wing on each side of the house had been carried up to the second story, and the arrangement of rooms was the same as below, outside stairways leading from the kitchens to the ground.

"I never saw so many beds in my life," cried Dorothy.

"Seems to be a perfect Bedlam," rejoined Harlan, making a poor attempt at a joke and laughing mirthlessly. In his heart he began to doubt the wisdom of marrying on six hundred dollars, an unexplored heirloom in Judson Centre, and an overweening desire to write books.

For the first time, his temerity appeared to him in its proper colours. He had been a space writer and Dorothy the private secretary of a Personage, when they met, in the dreary basement dining-room of a New York boarding-house, and speedily fell in love. Shortly afterward, when Harlan received a letter which contained a key, and announced that Mr. Judson's house, fully furnished, had been bequeathed to his nephew, they had light-heartedly embarked upon matrimony with no fears for the future.

Two hundred dollars had been spent upon a very modest honeymoon, and the three hundred and ninety-seven dollars and twenty-three cents remaining, as Harlan had accurately calculated, seemed pitifully small. Perplexity, doubt, and foreboding were plainly written on his face, when Dorothy turned to him.

"Isn't it perfectly lovely," she asked, "for us to have this nice, quiet place all to ourselves, where you can write your book?"

Woman-like, she had instantly touched the right chord, and the clouds vanished.

"Yes," he cried, eagerly. "Oh, Dorothy, do you think I can really write it?"

"Write it," she repeated; "why, you dear, funny goose, you can write a better book than anybody has ever written yet, and I know you can! By next week we'll be settled here and you can get down to work. I'll help you, too," she added, generously. "If you'll buy me a typewriter, I can copy the whole book for you."

"Of course I'll buy you a typewriter. We'll send for it to-morrow. How much does a nice one cost?"

"The kind I like," she explained, "costs a hundred dollars without the stand. I don't need the stand—we can find a table somewhere that will do."

"Two hundred and ninety-seven dollars and twenty-three cents," breathed Harlan, unconsciously.

"No, only a hundred dollars," corrected Dorothy. "I don't care to have it silver mounted."

"I'd buy you a gold one if you wanted it," stammered Harlan, in some confusion.

"Not now," she returned, serenely. "Wait till the book is done."

Visions of fame and fortune appeared before his troubled eyes and set his soul alight with high ambition. The candle in his hand burned unsteadily and dripped tallow, unheeded. "Come," said Dorothy, gently, "let's go downstairs again."

An open door revealed a tortuous stairway at the back of the house, descending mysteriously into cavernous gloom. "Let's go down here," she continued. "I love curly stairs."

"These are kinky enough to please even your refined fancy," laughed Harlan. "It reminds me of travelling in the West, where you look out of the window and see your engine on the track beside you, going the other way."

"This must be the kitchen," said Dorothy, when the stairs finally ceased. "Uncle Ebeneezer appears to have had a pronounced fancy for kitchens."

"Here's another wing," added Harlan, opening the back door. "Sitting-room, bedroom, and—my soul and body! It's another kitchen!"

"Any more beds?" queried Dorothy, peering into the darkness. "We can't keep house unless we can find more beds."

"Only one more. I guess we've come down to bed rock at last."

"In other words, the cradle," she observed, pulling a little old-fashioned trundle bed out into the light.

"Oh, what a joke!" cried Harlan. "That's worth three dollars in the office of any funny paper in New York!"

"Sell it," commanded Dorothy, inspired by the prospect of wealth, "and I'll give you fifty cents for your commission."

Outside, the storm still raged and the old house shook and creaked in the blast. The rain swirled furiously against the windows, and a swift rush of hailstones beat a fierce tattoo on the roof. Built on the summit of a hill and with only a few trees near it, the Judson mansion was but poorly protected from the elements.

None the less, there was a sense of warmth and comfort inside. "Let's build a fire in the kitchen," suggested Dorothy, "and then we'll try to find something to eat."

"Which kitchen?" asked Harlan.

"Any old kitchen. The one the back stairs end in, I guess. It seems to be the principal one of the set."

Harlan brought more wood and Dorothy watched him build the fire with a sense that a god-like being was here put to base uses. Hampered in his log-cabin design by the limitations of the fire box, he handled the kindlings awkwardly, got a splinter into his thumb, said something under his breath which was not meant for his wife to hear, and powdered his linen with soot from the stove pipe. At length, however, a respectable fire was started.

"Now," he asked, "what shall I do next?"

"Wind all the clocks. I can't endure a dead clock. While you're doing it, I'll get out the remnants of our lunch and see what there is in the pantry that is still edible."

In the lunch basket which the erratic ramifications of the road leading to Judson Centre had obliged them to carry, there was still, fortunately, a supply of sandwiches and fruit. A hasty search through the nearest pantry revealed jelly, marmalade, and pickles, a box of musty crackers and a canister of tea. When Harlan came back, Dorothy had the kitchen table set for two, with a lighted candle dispensing odorous good cheer from the centre of it, and the tea kettle singing merrily over the fire.

"Seems like home, doesn't it?" he asked, pleasantly imbued with the realisation of the home-making quality in Dorothy. Certain rare women with this gift take their atmosphere with them wherever they go.

"To-morrow," he went on, "I'll go into the village and buy more things to eat."

"The ruling passion," she smiled. "It's—what's that!"

Clear and high above the sound of the storm came an imperious "Me-ow!"

"It's a cat," said Harlan. "You don't suppose the poor thing is shut up anywhere, do you?"

"If it had been, we'd have found it. We've opened every door in the house, I'm sure. It must be outside."

"Me-ow! Me-ow! Me-ow!" The voice was not pleading; it was rather a command, a challenge.

"Kitty, kitty, kitty," she called. "Where are you, kitty?"

Harlan opened the outside door, and in rushed a huge black cat, with the air of one returning home after a long absence.

"Poor kitty," said Dorothy, kindly, stooping to stroke the sable visitor, who instinctively dodged the caress, and then scratched her hand.

"The ugly brute!" she exclaimed. "Don't touch him, Harlan."

Throughout the meal the cat sat at a respectful distance, with his greenish yellow eyes fixed unwaveringly upon them. He was entirely black, save for a white patch under his chin, which, in the half-light, carried with it an uncanny suggestion of a shirt front. Dorothy at length became restless under the calm scrutiny.

"I don't like him," she said. "Put him out."

"Thought you liked cats," remarked Harlan, reaching for another sandwich.

"I do, but I don't like this one. Please put him out."

"What, in all this storm? He'll get wet."

"He wasn't wet when he came in," objected Dorothy. "He must have some warm, dry place of his own outside."

"Come, kitty," said Harlan, pleasantly.

"Kitty" merely blinked, and Harlan rose.

"Come, kitty."

With the characteristic independence of cats, the visitor yawned. The conversation evidently bored him.

"Come, kitty," said Harlan, more firmly, with a low swoop of his arm. The cat arched his back, erected an enlarged tail, and hissed threateningly. In a dignified but effective manner, he eluded all attempts to capture him, even avoiding Dorothy and her broom.

"There's something more or less imperial about him," she remarked, wiping her flushed cheeks, when they had finally decided not to put the cat out. "As long as he's adopted us, we'll have to keep him. What shall we name him?"

"Claudius Tiberius," answered Harlan. "It suits him down to the ground."

"His first name is certainly appropriate," laughed Dorothy, with a rueful glance at her scratched hand. Making the best of a bad bargain, she spread an old grey shawl, nicely folded, on the floor by the stove, and requested Claudius Tiberius to recline upon it, but he persistently ignored the invitation.

"This is jolly enough," said Harlan. "A cosy little supper in our own house, with a gale blowing outside, the tea kettle singing over the fire, and a cat purring on the hearth."

"Have you heard Claudius purr?" asked Dorothy, idly.

"Come to think of it, I haven't. Perhaps something is wrong with his purrer. We'll fix him to-morrow."

From a remote part of the house came twelve faint, silvery tones. The kitchen clock struck next, with short, quick strokes, followed immediately by a casual record of the hour from the clock on the mantel beneath Uncle Ebeneezer's portrait. Then the grandfather's clock in the hall boomed out twelve, solemn funereal chimes. Afterward, the silence seemed acute.

"The end of the honeymoon," said Dorothy, a little sadly, with a quick, inquiring look at her husband.

"The end of the honeymoon!" repeated Harlan, gathering her into his arms. "To-morrow, life begins!"

Several hours later, Dorothy awoke from a dreamless sleep to wonder whether life was any different from a honeymoon, and if so, how and why.

# II

## The Day Afterward

By the pitiless light of early morning, the house was even uglier than at night. With an irreverence essentially modern, Dorothy decided, while she was dressing, to have all the furniture taken out into the back yard, where she could look it over at her leisure. She would make a bonfire of most of it, or, better yet, have it cut into wood for the fireplace. Thus Uncle Ebeneezer's cumbrous bequest might be quickly transformed into comfort.

"And," thought Dorothy, "I'll take down that hideous portrait over the mantel before I'm a day older."

But when she broached the subject to Harlan, she found him unresponsive and somewhat disinclined to interfere with the existing order of things. "We'll be here only for the Summer," he said, "so what's the use of monkeying with the furniture and burning up fifty or sixty beds? There's plenty of wood in the cellar."

"I don't like the furniture," she pouted.

"My dear," said Harlan, with patronising kindness, "as you grow older, you'll find lots of things on the planet which you don't like. Moreover, it'll be quite out of your power to cremate 'em, and it's just as well to begin adjusting yourself now."

This bit of philosophy irritated Mrs. Carr unbearably. "Do you mean to say," she demanded, with rising temper, "that you won't do as I ask you to?"

"Do you mean to say," inquired Harlan, wickedly, in exact imitation of her manner, "that you won't do as I ask you to? Four weeks ago yesterday, if I remember rightly, you promised to obey me!"

"Don't remind me of what I'm ashamed of!" flashed Dorothy. "If I'd known what a brute you were, I'd never have married you! You may be sure of that!"

Claudius Tiberius insinuated himself between Harlan's feet and rubbed against his trousers, leaving a thin film of black fur in his wake. Being fastidious about his personal appearance, Harlan kicked Claudius Tiberius vigorously, grabbed his hat and went out, slamming the door, and whistling with an exaggerated cheerfulness.

"Brute!" The word rankled deeply as he went downhill with his hands in his pockets, whistling determinedly. So Dorothy was sorry she had married him!

After all he'd done for her, too. Giving up a good position in New York, taking her half-way around the world on a honeymoon, and bringing her to a magnificent country residence in a fashionable locality for the Summer!

Safely screened by the hill, he turned back to look at the "magnificent country residence," then swore softly under his breath, as, for the first time, he took in the full meaning of the eccentric architecture.

Perched high upon the hill, with intervening shrubbery carefully cut down, the Judson mansion was not one to inspire confidence in its possessor. Outwardly, it was grey and weather-worn, with the shingles dropping off in places. At the sides, the rambling wings and outside stairways, branching off into space, conveyed the impression that the house had been recently subjected to a powerful influence f the centrifugal sort. But worst of all was the front elevation, with its two round windows, its narrow, long window in the centre, and the low windows on either side of the front door—the grinning, distorted semblance of a human face.

The bare, uncurtained windows loomed up boldly in the searching sunlight, which spared nothing. The blue smoke rising from the kitchen chimney appeared strangely like a plume streaming out from the rear. Harlan noted, too, that the railing of the narrow porch extended almost entirely across the front of the house, and remembered, dimly, that they had found the steps at one side of the porch the night before. Not a single unpleasant detail was in any way hidden, and he clutched instinctively at a tree as he realised that the supports of the railing were cunningly arranged to look like huge teeth.

"No wonder," he said to himself "that the stage driver called it the Jack-o'-Lantern! That's exactly what it is! Why didn't he paint it yellow and be done with it? The old devil!" The last disrespectful allusion, of course, being meant for Uncle Ebeneezer.

"Poor Dorothy," he thought again. "I'll burn the whole thing, and she shall put every blamed crib into the purifying flames. It's mine, and I can do what I please with it. We'll go away to-morrow, we'll go——"

Where could they go, with less than four hundred dollars? Especially when one hundred of it was promised for a typewriter? Harlan had parted with his managing editor on terms of great dignity, announcing that he had forsworn journalism and would hereafter devote himself to literature. The editor had remarked, somewhat cynically, that it was a better day for journalism than for literature, the fine, inner meaning of the retort not having been fully evident to Harlan until he was some three squares away from the office.

Much chastened in spirit, and fully ready to accept his wife's estimate of him, he went on downhill into Judson Centre.

It was the usual small town, the post-office, grocery, meat market, and general loafing-place being combined under one roof. Near by was the blacksmith shop, and across from it was the inevitable saloon. Far up in the hills was the Judson Centre Sanitarium, a worthy institution of some years standing, where every human ailment from tuberculosis to fits was more or less successfully treated.

Upon the inmates of the sanitarium the inhabitants of Judson Centre lived, both materially and mentally. Few of them had ever been nearer to it than the back door, but tales of dark doings were widely prevalent throughout the community, and mothers were wont to frighten their young offspring into obedience with threats of the "san-tor-i-yum."

"Now what do you reckon ails *him*?" asked the blacksmith of the stage-driver, as Harlan went into the village store.

"Wouldn't reckon nothin' ailed him to look at him, would you?" queried the driver, in reply.

Indeed, no one looking at Mr. Carr would have suspected him of an "ailment." He was tall and broad-shouldered and well set up, with clear grey eyes and a rosy, smooth-shaven, boyish face which had given him the nickname of "The Cherub" all along Newspaper Row. In his bearing there was a suggestion of boundless energy, which needed only proper direction to accomplish wonders.

"You can't never tell," continued the driver, shifting his quid. "Now, I've took folks up there goin' on ten year now, an' some I've took up looked considerable more healthy than I be when I took 'em up. Comin' back, howsumever, it was different. One young feller rode up with me in the rain one night, a-singin' an' a-whistlin' to beat the band, an' when I took him back, a month or so arterward, he had a striped nurse on one side of him an' a doctor on t' other, an' was wearin' a shawl. Couldn't hardly set up, but he was a-tryin' to joke just the same. 'Hank,' says he, when we got a little way off from the place, 'my book of life has been edited by the librarians an' the entire appendix removed.' Them's his very words. 'An',' says he, 'the time to have the appendix took out is before it does much of anythin' to your table of contents.'

"The doctor shut him up then, an' I didn't hear no more, but I remembered the language, an' arterwards, when I got a chanst, I looked in the school-teacher's dictionary. It said as how the appendix was sunthin' appended or added to, but I couldn't get no more about it. I've hearn tell of a 'devil child' with a tail to it what was travellin' with the circus one year, an' I've surmised as how mebbe a tail had begun to grow on this young feller an' it was took off."

"You don't say!" ejaculated the blacksmith.

By reason of his professional connection with the sanitarium, Mr. Henry Blake was, in a sense, the oracle of Judson Centre, and he enjoyed his proud distinction to the full. Ordinarily, he was taciturn, but the present hour found him in a conversational mood.

"He's married," he went on, returning to the original subject. "I took him an' his wife up to the Jack-o'-Lantern last night. Come in on the nine forty-seven from the Junction. Reckon they're goin' to stay a spell, 'cause they've got trunks—one of a reasonable size, an' 'nother that looks like a dog-house. Box, too, that's got lead in it."

"Books, maybe," suggested the blacksmith, with unexpected discernment. "Schoolteacher boarded to our house wunst an' she had most a car-load of 'em. Educated folks has to have books to keep from losin' their education."

"Don't take much stock in it myself," remarked the driver. "It spiles most folks. As soon as they get some, they begin to pine an' hanker for more. I knowed a feller wunst that begun with one book dropped on the road near the sanitarium, an' he never stopped till he was plum through college. An' a woman up there sent my darter a book wunst, an' I took it right back to her. 'My darter's got a book,' says I, 'an' she ain't a-needin' of no duplicates. Keep it,' says I, 'fer somebody that ain't got no book."

"Do you reckon," asked the blacksmith, after a long silence, "that they're goin' to live in the Jack-o'-Lantern?"

"I ain't a-sayin'," answered Mr. Blake, cautiously. "They're educated, an' there's no tellin' what educated folks is goin' to do. This young lady, now, that come up with him last night, she said it was 'a dear old place an' she loved it a'ready.' Them's her very words!"

"Do tell!"

"That's c'rrect, an' as I said before, when you're dealin' with educated folks, you're swimmin' in deep water with the shore clean out o' sight. Education was what ailed him." By a careless nod Mr. Blake indicated the Jack-o'-Lantern, which could be seen from the main thoroughfare of Judson Centre.

"I've hearn," he went on, taking a fresh bite from his morning purchase of "plug," "that he had one hull room mighty nigh plum full o' nothin' but books, an' there was always more comin' by freight an' express an' through the post-office. It's all on account o' them books that he's made the front o' his house into what it is. My wife had a paper book wunst, a-tellin' 'How to Transfer a Hopeless Exterior,' with pictures of houses in it like they be here an' more arter they'd been transferred. You bet I burnt it while she was gone to sewin' circle, an' there ain't no book come into my house since."

Mr. Blake spoke with the virtuous air of one who has protected his home from contamination. Indeed, as he had often said before, "you can't never tell what folks'll do when books gets a holt of 'em."

"Do you reckon," asked the blacksmith, "that there'll be company?"

"Company," snickered Mr. Blake, "oh, my Lord, yes! A little thing like death ain't never going to keep company away. Ain't you never hearn as how misery loves company? The more miserable you are the more company you'll have, an' vice versey, etcetery an' the same."

"Hush!" warned the blacksmith, in a harsh whisper. "He's a-comin'!"

"City feller," grumbled Mr. Blake, affecting not to see.

"Good-morning," said Harlan, pleasantly, though not without an air of condescension. "Can you tell me where I can find the stage-driver?"

"That's me," grunted Mr. Blake. "Be you wantin' anythin'?"

"Only to pay you for taking us up to the house last night, and to arrange about our trunks. Can you deliver them this afternoon?"

"I ain't a-runnin' of no livery, but I can take 'em up, if that's what you're wantin'."

"Exactly," said Harlan, "and the box, too, if you will. And the things I've just ordered at the grocery—can you bring them, too?"

Mr. Blake nodded helplessly, and the blacksmith gazed at Harlan, open-mouthed, as he started uphill. "Must sure have a ailment," he commented, "but I hear tell, Hank, that in the city they never carry nothin' round with 'em but perhaps an umbrell. Everythin' else they have 'sent.'"

"Reckon it's true enough. I took a ham wunst up to the sanitarium for a young sprig of a doctor that was too proud to carry it himself. He was goin' that way, too—walkin' up to save money—so I charged him for carryin' up the ham just what I'd have took both for. 'Pigs is high,' I told him, 'same price for one as for 'nother,' but he didn't pay no attention to it an' never raised no kick about the price. Thinkin' 'bout sunthin' else, most likely—most of 'em are."

Harlan, most assuredly, was "thinkin' 'bout sunthin' else." In fact, he was possessed by portentous uneasiness. There was well-defined doubt in his mind regarding his reception at the Jack-o'-Lantern. Dorothy's parting words had been plain—almost to the point of rudeness, he reflected, unhappily, and he was not sure that "a brute" would be allowed in her presence again.

The bare, uncurtained windows gave no sign of human occupancy. Perhaps she had left him! Then his reason came to the rescue—there was no way for her to go but downhill, and he would certainly have seen her had she taken that path.

When he entered the yard, he smelled smoke, and ran wildly into the house. A hasty search through all the rooms revealed nothing—even Dorothy had

16

disappeared. From the kitchen window, he saw her in the back yard, poking idly through a heap of smouldering rubbish with an old broomstick.

"What are you doing?" he demanded, breathlessly, before she knew he was near her.

Dorothy turned, disguising her sudden start by a toss of her head. "Oh," she said, coolly, "it's you, is it?"

Harlan bit his lips and his eyes laughed. "I say, Dorothy," he began, awkwardly; "I was rather a beast, wasn't I?"

"Of course," she returned, in a small, unnatural voice, still poking through the ruins. "I told you so, didn't I?"

"I didn't believe you at the time," Harlan went on, eager to make amends, "but I do now."

"That's good." Mrs. Carr's tone was not at all reassuring.

There was an awkward pause, then Harlan, putting aside his obstinate pride, said the simple sentence which men of all ages have found it hardest to say— perhaps because it is the sign of utter masculine abasement. "I'm sorry, dear, will you forgive me?"

In a moment, she was in his arms. "It was partly my fault," she admitted, generously, from the depths of his coat collar. "I think there must be something in the atmosphere of the house. We never quarrelled before."

"And we never will again," answered Harlan, confidently. "What have you been burning?"

"It was a mattress," whispered Dorothy, much ashamed. "I tried to get a bed out, but it was too heavy."

"You funny, funny girl! How did you ever get a mattress out, all alone?"

"Dragged it to an upper window and dumped it," she explained, blushing, "then came down and dragged it some more. Claudius Tiberius didn't like to have me do it."

"I don't wonder," laughed Harlan. "That is," he added hastily, "he couldn't have been pleased to see you doing it all by yourself. Anybody would love to see a mattress burn."

"Shall we get some more? There are plenty."

"Let's not take all our pleasure at once," he suggested, with rare tact. "One mattress a day—how'll that do?"

"We'll have it at night," cried Dorothy, clapping her hands, "and when the mattresses are all gone, we'll do the beds and bureaus and the haircloth furniture in the parlour. Oh, I do so love a bonfire!"

17

Harlan's heart grew strangely tender, for it had been this underlying childishness in her that he had loved the most. She was stirring the ashes now, with as much real pleasure as though she were five instead of twenty-five.

As it happened, Harlan would have been saved a great deal of trouble if he had followed out her suggestion and burned all of the beds in the house except two or three, but the balance between foresight and retrospection has seldom been exact.

"Beast of a smudge you're making," he commented, choking.

"Get around to the other side, then. Why, Harlan, what's that?"

"What's what?"

She pointed to a small metal box in the midst of the ashes.

"Poem on Spring, probably, put into the corner-stone by the builder of the mattress."

"Don't be foolish," she said, with assumed severity. "Get me a pail of water."

With two sticks they lifted it into the water and waited, impatiently enough, until they were sure it was cool. Then Dorothy, asserting her right of discovery, opened it with trembling fingers.

"Why-ee!" she gasped.

Upon a bed of wet cotton lay a large brooch, made wholly of clustered diamonds, and a coral necklace, somewhat injured by the fire.

"Whose is it?" demanded Dorothy, when she recovered the faculty of speech.

"I should say," returned Harlan, after due deliberation, "that it belonged to you."

"After this," she said, slowly, her eyes wide with wonder, "we'll take everything apart before we burn it."

Harlan was turning the brooch over in his hand and roughly estimating its value at two thousand dollars. "Here's something on the back," he said. "'R. from E., March , .'"

"Rebecca from Ebeneezer," cried Dorothy. "Oh, Harlan, it's ours! Don't you remember the letter said: 'my house and all its contents to my beloved nephew, James Harlan Carr'?"

"I remember," said Harlan. But his conscience was uneasy, none the less.

# III

# The First Caller

As Mr. Blake had heard, there was "one hull room mighty nigh plum full o' nothin' but books"; a grievous waste, indeed, when one already "had a book." It was the front room, opposite the parlour, and every door and window in it could be securely bolted from the inside. If any one desired unbroken privacy, it could be had in the library as nowhere else in the house.

The book-shelves were made of rough pine, unplaned, unpainted, and were scarcely a seemly setting for the treasure they bore. But in looking at the books, one perceived that their owner had been one who passed by the body in his eager search for the soul.

Here were no fine editions, no luxurious, costly volumes in full levant. Illuminated pages, rubricated headings, and fine illustrations were conspicuous by their absence. For the most part, the books were simply but serviceably bound in plain cloth covers. Many a paper-covered book had been bound by its purchaser in pasteboard, flimsy enough in quality, yet further strengthened by cloth at the back. Cheap, pirated editions were so many that Harlan wondered whether his uncle had not been wholly without conscience in the matter of book-buying.

Shelf after shelf stretched across the long wall, with its company of mute consolers whose master was no more. The fine flowering of the centuries, like a single precious drop of imperishable perfume, was hidden in this rude casket. The minds and hearts of the great, laid pitilessly bare, were here in this one room, shielded merely by pasteboard and cloth.

Far up in the mountains, amid snow-clad steeps and rock-bound fastnesses, one finds, perchance, a shell. It is so small a thing that it can be held in the hollow of the hand; so frail that a slight pressure of the finger will crush it to atoms, yet, held to the ear, it brings the surge and sweep of that vast, primeval ocean which, in the inconceivably remote past, covered the peak. And so, to the eye of the mind, the small brown book, with its hundred printed pages, brings back the whole story of the world.

A thin, piping voice, to which its fellows have paid no heed, after a time becomes silent, and, ceaselessly marching, the years pass on by. Yet that trembling old hand, quietly laid at last upon the turbulent heart, in the solitude of a garret has guided a pen, and the manuscript is left. Ragged, worn, blotted, spotted with candle drippings and endlessly interlined, why should these few sheets of paper be saved?

Because, as it happens, the only record of the period is there—a record so significant that fifty years can be reconstructed, as an entire language was brought to light by a triple inscription upon a single stone. Thrown like the shell upon Time's ever-receding shore, it is, nevertheless, the means by which unborn thousands shall commune with him who wrote in his garret, see his whole life mirrored in his book, know his philosophy, and take home his truth. For by way of the printed page comes Immortality.

There was no book in the library which had not been read many times. Some were falling apart, and others had been carefully sewn together and awkwardly rebound. Still open, on a rickety table in the corner, was that ponderous volume with an extremely limited circulation: *The Publishers' Trade List Annual*. Pencilled crosses here and there indicated books to be purchased, or at least sent on approval, to "customers known to the House."

"Some day," said Dorothy, "when it's raining and we can't go out, we'll take down all these books, arrange them in something like order, and catalogue them."

"How optimistic you are!" remarked Harlan. "Do you think it could be done in one day?"

"Oh, well," returned Dorothy; "you know what I mean."

Harlan paced restlessly back and forth, pausing now and then to look out of the window, where nothing much was to be seen except the orchard, at a little distance from the house, and Claudius Tiberius, sunning himself pleasantly upon the porch. Four weeks had been a pleasant vacation, but two weeks of comparative idleness, added to it, were too much for an active mind and body to endure. Three or four times he had tried to begin the book that was to bring fame and fortune, and as many times had failed. Hitherto Harlan's work had not been obliged to wait for inspiration, and it was not so easy as it had seemed the day he bade his managing editor farewell.

"Somebody is coming," announced Dorothy, from the window.

"Nonsense! Nobody ever comes here."

"A precedent is about to be established, then. I feel it in my bones that we're going to have company."

"Let's see." Harlan went to the window and looked over her shoulder. A little man in a huge silk hat was toiling up the hill, aided by a cane. He was bent and old, yet he moved with a certain briskness, and, as Dorothy had said, he was inevitably coming.

"Who in thunder—" began Harlan.

"Our first company," interrupted Dorothy, with her hand over his mouth. "The very first person who has called on us since we were married!"

"Except Claudius Tiberius," amended Harlan. "Isn't a cat anybody?"

"Claudius is. I beg his imperial pardon for forgetting him."

The rusty bell-wire creaked, then a timid ring came from the rear depths of the house. "You let him in," said Dorothy, "and I'll go and fix my hair."

"Am I right," queried the old gentleman, when Harlan opened the door, "in presuming that I am so fortunate as to address Mr. James Harlan Carr?"

"My name is Carr," answered Harlan, politely. "Will you come in?"

"Thank you," answered the visitor, in high staccato, oblivious of the fact that Claudius Tiberius had scooted in between his feet; "it will be my pleasure to claim your hospitality for a few brief moments.

"I had hoped," he went on, as Harlan ushered him into the parlour, "to be able to make your acquaintance before this, but my multitudinous duties——"

He fumbled in his pocket and produced a card, cut somewhat irregularly from a sheet of white cardboard, and bearing in tremulous autographic script: "Jeremiah Bradford, Counsellor at Law."

"Oh," said Harlan, "it was you who wrote me the letter. I should have hunted you up when I first came, shouldn't I?"

"Not at all," returned Mr. Bradford. "It is I who have been remiss. It is etiquette that the old residents should call first upon the newcomers. Many and varied duties in connection with the practice of my profession have hitherto—" His eyes sought the portrait over the mantel. "A most excellent likeness of your worthy uncle," he continued, irrelevantly, "a gentleman with whom, as I understand, you never had the pleasure and privilege of becoming acquainted."

"I never met Uncle Ebeneezer," rejoined Harlan, "but mother told me a great deal about him and we had one or two pictures—daguerreotypes, I believe they were."

"Undoubtedly, my dear sir. This portrait was painted from his very last daguerreotype by an artist of renown. It is a wonderful likeness. He was my Colonel—I served under him in the war. It was my desire to possess a portrait of him in uniform, but he would never consent, and would not allow anyone save myself to address him as Colonel. An eccentric, but very estimable gentleman."

"I cannot understand," said Harlan, "why he should have left the house to me. I had never even seen him."

"Perhaps," smiled Mr. Bradford, enigmatically, "that was his reason, or rather, perhaps I should say, if you had known your uncle more intimately and had visited him here, or, if he had had the privilege of knowing you—quite often, as you know, a personal acquaintance proves disappointing, though, of course, in this case——"

The old gentleman was floundering helplessly when Harlan rescued him. "I want you to meet my wife, Mr. Bradford. If you will excuse me, I will call her."

Left to himself, the visitor slipped back and forth uneasily upon his haircloth chair, and took occasion to observe Claudius Tiberius, who sat near by and regarded the guest unblinkingly. Hearing approaching footsteps, he took out his worn silk handkerchief, unfolded it, and wiped the cold perspiration from his legal brow. In his heart of hearts, he wished he had not come, but Dorothy's kindly greeting at once relieved him of all embarrassment.

"We have been wondering," she said, brightly, "who would be the first to call upon us, and you have come at exactly the right time. New residents are always given two weeks, are they not, in which to get settled?"

"Quite so, my dear madam, quite so, and I trust that you are by this time fully accustomed to your changed environment. Judson Centre, while possessing few metropolitan advantages, has distinct and peculiar recommendations of an individual character which endear the locality to those residing therein."

"I think I shall like it here," said Dorothy. "At least I shall try to."

"A very commendable spirit," rejoined the old gentleman, warmly, "and rather remarkable in one so young."

Mrs. Carr graciously acknowledged the compliment, and the guest flushed with pleasure. To perception less fine, there would have been food for unseemly mirth in his attire. Never in all her life before had Dorothy seen rough cow-hide boots, and grey striped trousers worn with a rusty and moth-eaten dress-coat in the middle of the afternoon. An immaculate expanse of shirt-front and a general air of extreme cleanliness went far toward redeeming the unfamiliar costume. The silk hat, with a bell-shaped crown and wide, rolling brim, belonged to a much earlier period, and had been brushed to look like new. Even Harlan noted that the ravelled edges of his linen had been carefully trimmed and the worn binding of the hat brim inked wherever necessary.

His wrinkled old face was kindly, though somewhat sad. His weak blue eyes were sheltered by an enormous pair of spectacles, which he took off and wiped continually. He was smooth-shaven and his scanty hair was as white as the driven snow. Now, as he sat in Uncle Ebeneezer's parlour, he seemed utterly friendless and forlorn—a complete failure of that pitiful type which never for a moment guesses that it has failed.

"It will be my delight," the old man was saying, his hollow cheeks faintly flushed, "to see that the elite of Judson Centre pay proper respect to you at an early date. If I were not most unfortunately a single gentleman, my wife would do herself the honour of calling upon you immediately and of tendering you some sort of hospitality approximately commensurate with your worth. As it is——"

"As it is," said Harlan, taking up the wandering thread of the discourse, "that particular pleasure must be on our side. We both hope that you will come often, and informally."

"It would be a solace to me," rejoined the old gentleman, tremulously, "to find the niece and nephew of my departed friend both congenial and companionable. He was my Colonel—I served under him in the war—and until the last, he allowed me to address him as Colonel—a privilege accorded to no one else. He very seldom left his own estate, but at his request I often spent an evening or a Sunday afternoon in his society, and after his untimely death, I feel the loss of his companionship very keenly. He was my Colonel—I——"

"I should imagine so," said Harlan, kindly, "though, as I have told you, I never knew him at all."

"A much-misunderstood gentleman," continued Mr. Bradford, carefully wiping his spectacles. "My grief is too recent, at present, to enable me to discourse freely of his many virtues, but at some future time I shall hope to make you acquainted with your benefactor. He was my Colonel, and in serving under him in the war, I had an unusual pportunity to know him as he really was. May I ask, without intruding upon your private affairs, whether or not it is your intention to reside here permanently?"

"We have not made up our minds," responded Harlan. "We shall stay here this Summer, anyway, as I have some work to do which can be done only in a quiet place."

"Quiet!" muttered the old gentleman, "quiet place! If I might venture to suggest, I should think you would find any other season more agreeable for prolonged mental effort. In Summer there are distractions——"

"Yes," put in Dorothy, "in Summer, one wants to be outdoors, and I am going to keep chickens and a cow, but my husband hopes to have his book finished by September."

"His book!" repeated Mr. Bradford, in genuine astonishment. "Am I actually addressing an author?"

He beamed upon Harlan in a way which that modest youth found positively disconcerting.

"A would-be author only," laughed Harlan, the colour mounting to his temples. "I've done newspaper work heretofore, and now I'm going to try something else."

"My dear sir," said Mr. Bradford, rising, "I must really beg the privilege of clasping your hand. It is a great honour for Judson Centre to have an author residing in its midst!"

Taking pity upon Harlan, Dorothy hastened to change the subject. "We hope it may be," she observed, lightly, "and I wonder, Mr. Bradford, if you could not give me some good advice?"

"I shall be delighted, my dear madam. Any knowledge I may possess is trebly at your service, for the sake of the distinguished author whose wife you have the honour to be, for the sake of your departed relative, who was my friend, my Colonel, and last, but not least, for your own sake."

"It is only about a maid," said Dorothy.

"A —— my dear madam, I beg your pardon?"

"A maid," repeated Dorothy; "a servant."

"Oh! A hired girl, or more accurately, in the parlance of Judson Centre, the help. Do I understand that it is your desire to become an employer of help?"

"It is," answered Dorothy, somewhat awed by the solemnity of his tone, "if help is to be found. I thought you might know where I could get some one."

"If I might be permitted to suggest," replied Mr. Bradford, after due deliberation, "I should unhesitatingly recommend Mrs. Sarah Smithers, who did for your uncle during the entire period of his residence here and whose privilege it was to close his eyes in his last sleep. She is at present without prospect of a situation, and I believe would be very ready to accept a new position, especially so desirable a position as this, in your service."

"Thank you. Could you—could you send her to me?"

"I shall do so, most assuredly, providing she is willing to come, and should she chance not to be agreeably disposed toward so pleasing a project, it will be my happiness to endeavour to persuade her." Drawing out a memorandum book and a pencil, the old gentleman made an entry upon a fresh page. "The multitudinous duties in connection with the practice of my profession," he began—"there, my dear madam, it is already attended to, since it is placed quite out of my power to forget."

"I am greatly obliged," said Dorothy.

"And now," continued the visitor, "I must go. I fear I have already outstayed the limitation of a formal visit, such as the first should be, and it is not my desire to intrude upon an author's time. Moreover, my own duties, slight and unimportant as they are in comparison, must ultimately press upon my attention."

"Come again," said Harlan, kindly, following him to the door.

"It will be my great pleasure," rejoined the guest, "not only on your own account, but because your personality reminds me of that of my departed friend. You favour him considerably, more particularly in the eyes, if I may be permitted to allude to details. I think I told you, did I not, that he was my Colonel and I was privileged to serve under him in the war? My—oh, I walked, did I not? I remember that it was my intention to come in a carriage, as being more suitable to a formal visit, but Mr. Blake had other engagements for his vehicle. Dear sir and madam, I bid you good afternoon."

So saying, he went downhill, briskly enough, yet stumbling where the way was rough. They watched him until the bobbing, bell-shaped crown of the ancient head-gear was completely out of sight.

"What a dear old man!" said Dorothy. "He's lonely and we must have him come up often."

"Do you think," asked Harlan, "that I look like Uncle Ebeneezer?"

"Indeed you don't!" cried Dorothy, "and that reminds me. I want to take that picture down."

"To burn it?" inquired Harlan, slyly.

"No, I wouldn't burn it," answered Dorothy, somewhat spitefully, "but there's no law against putting it in the attic, is there?"

"Not that I know of. Can we reach it from a chair?"

Together they mounted one of the haircloth monuments, slipping, as Dorothy said, until it was like walking on ice.

"Now then," said Harlan, gaily, "come on down, Uncle! You're about to be moved into the attic!"

The picture lunged forward, almost before they had touched it, the heavy gilt frame bruising Dorothy's cheek badly. In catching it, Harlan turned it completely around, then gave a low whistle of astonishment.

Pasted securely to the back was a fearsome skull and cross-bones, made on wrapping paper with a brush and India ink. Below it, in great capitals, was the warning inscription: "LET MY PICTURE ALONE!"

"What shall we do with it?" asked Harlan, endeavouring to laugh, though, as he afterward admitted, he "felt creepy." "Shall I take it up to the attic?"

"No," answered Dorothy, in a small, unnatural voice, "leave it where it is."

While Harlan was putting it back, Dorothy, trembling from head to foot, crept around to the back of the easel which bore Aunt Rebecca's portrait. She was not at all surprised to find, on the back of it, a notice to this effect: "ANYONE

DARING TO MOVE MRS. JUDSON'S PICTURE WILL BE HAUNTED
FOR LIFE BY US BOTH."

"I don't doubt it," said Dorothy, somewhat viciously, when Harlan had joined
her. "What kind of a woman do you suppose she could have been, to marry
him? I'll bet she's glad she's dead!"

Dorothy was still wiping blood from her face and might not have been wholly
unprejudiced. Aunt Rebecca was a gentle, sweet-faced woman, if her portrait
told the truth, possessed of all the virtues save self-assertion and dominated by
habitual, unselfish kindness to others. She could not have been discourteous
even to Claudius Tiberius, who at this moment was seated in state upon the
sofa and purring industriously.

# IV

## Finances

"I've ordered the typewriter," said Dorothy, brightly, "and some nice new note-paper, and a seal. I've just been reading about making virtue out of necessity, so I've ordered 'At the Sign of the Jack-o'-Lantern' put on our stationery, in gold, and a yellow pumpkin on the envelope flap, just above the seal. And I want you to make a funny sign-board to flap from a pole, the way they did in 'Rudder Grange.' If you could make a wooden Jack-o'-Lantern, we could have a candle inside it at night, and then the sign would be just like the house. We can get the paint and things down in the village. Won't it be cute? We're farmers, now, so we'll have to pretend we like it."

Harlan repressed an exclamation, which could not have been wholly inspired by pleasure.

"What's the matter?" asked Dorothy, easily. "Don't you like the design for the note-paper? If you don't, you won't have to use it. Nobody's going to make you write letters on paper you don't like, so cheer up."

"It isn't the paper," answered Harlan, miserably; "it's the typewriter." Up to the present moment, sustained by a false, but none the less determined pride, he had refrained from taking his wife into his confidence regarding his finances. With characteristic masculine short-sightedness, he had failed to perceive that every moment of delay made matters worse.

"Might I inquire," asked Mrs. Carr, coolly, "what is wrong with the typewriter?"

"Nothing at all," sighed Harlan, "except that we can't afford it." The whole bitter truth was out, now, and he turned away wretchedly, ashamed to meet her eyes.

It seemed ages before she spoke. Then she said, in smooth, icy tones: "What was your object in offering to get it for me?"

"I spoke impulsively," explained Harlan, forgetting that he had never suggested buying a typewriter. "I didn't stop to think. I'm sorry," he concluded, lamely.

"I suppose you spoke impulsively," snapped Dorothy, "when you asked me to marry you. You're sorry for that, too, aren't you?"

"Dorothy!"

"You're not the only one who's sorry," she rejoined, her cheeks flushed and her eyes blazing. "I had no idea what an expense I was going to be!"

"Dorothy!" cried Harlan, angrily; "you didn't think I was a millionaire, did you? Were you under the impression that I was an active branch of the United States Mint?"

"No," she answered, huskily; "I merely thought I was marrying a gentleman instead of a loafer, and I beg your pardon for the mistake!" She slammed the door on the last word, and he heard her light feet pattering swiftly down the hall, little guessing that she was trying to gain the shelter of her own room before giving way to a tempest of sobs.

Happy are they who can drown all pain, sorrow, and disappointment in a copious flood of tears. In an hour, at the most, Dorothy would be her sunny self again, penitent, and wholly ashamed of her undignified outburst. By to-morrow she would have forgotten it, but Harlan, made of sterner clay, would remember it for days.

"Loafer!" The cruel word seemed written accusingly on every wall of the room. In a sudden flash of insight he perceived the truth of it—and it hurt.

"Two months," bethought; "two months of besotted idleness. And I used to chase news from the Battery to the Bronx every day from eight to six! Murders, smallpox, East Side scraps, and Tammany Hall. Why in the hereafter can't they have a fire at the sanitarium, or something that I can wire in?"

"The Temple of Healing," as Dorothy had christened it in a happier moment, stood on a distant hill, all but hidden now by trees and shrubbery. A column of smoke curled lazily upward against the blue, but there was no immediate prospect of a fire of the "news" variety.

Harlan stood at the window for a long time, deeply troubled. The call of the city dinned relentlessly into his ears. Oh, for an hour in the midst of it, with the rumble and roar and clatter of ceaseless traffic, the hurrying, heedless throng rushing in every direction, the glare of the sun on the many-windowed cliffs, the fever of the struggle in his veins!

And yet—was two months so long, when a fellow was just married, and hadn't had more than a day at a time off for six years? Since the "cub reporter" was first "licked into shape" in the office of *The Thunderer*, there had been plenty of work for him, year in and year out.

"I wonder," he mused, "if the old man would take me back on my job?"

"I can see 'em in the office now," went on Harlan, mentally, "when I go back and tell 'em I want my place again. The old man will look up and say: 'The hell you do! Thought you'd accepted a position on the literary circuit as manager of the nine muses! Better run along and look after 'em before they join the union.'

"And the exchange man will yell at me not to slam the door as I go out, and I'll be pointed out to the newest kid as a horrible example of misdirected ambition. Brinkman will say: 'Sonny, there's a bloke that got too good for his job and now he's come back, willing to edit The Mother's Corner.'

"It'd be about the same in the other offices, too," he thought. "'Sorry, nothing to-day, but there might be next month. Drop in again sometime after six weeks or so and meanwhile I'll let you know if anything turns up. Yes, I can remember your address. Don't slam the door as you go out. Most people seem to have been born in a barn.'

"Besides," he continued to himself, fiercely, "what is there in it? They'll take your youth, all your strength and energy, and give you a measly living in exchange. They'll fill you with excitement till you're never good for anything else, any more than a cavalry horse is fitted to pull a vegetable wagon. Then, when you're old, they've got no use for you!"

Before his mental vision, in pitiful array, came that unhappy procession of hacks that files, day in and day out, along Newspaper Row, drawn by every instinct to the arena that holds nothing for them but a meagre, uncertain pittance, dwindling slowly to charity.

"That's where I'd be at the last of it," muttered Harlan, savagely, "with even the cubs offering me the price of a drink to get out. And Dorothy—good God! Where would Dorothy be?"

He clenched his fists and marched up and down the room in utter despair. "Why," he breathed, "why wasn't I taught to do something honest, instead of being cursed with this itch to write? A carpenter, a bricklayer, a stone-mason,—any one of 'em has a better chance than I!"

And yet, even then, Harlan saw clearly that save where some vast cathedral reared its unnumbered spires, the mason and the bricklayer were without significance; that even the builders were remembered only because of the great uses to which their buildings were put. "That, too, through print," he murmured. "It all comes down to the printed page at last."

On a table, near by, was a sheaf of rough copy paper, and six or eight carefully sharpened pencils—the dull, meaningless stone waiting for the flint that should strike it into flame. Day after day the table had stood by the window, without result, save in Harlan's uneasy conscience.

"I'm only a tramp," he said, aloud, "and I've known it, all along."

He sat down by the table and took up a pencil, but no words came. Remorsefully, he wrote to an acquaintance—a man who had a book published every year and filled in the intervening time with magazine work and newspaper specials. He sealed the letter and addressed it idly, then tossed it aside purposelessly.

"Loafer!" The memory of it stung him like a lash, and, completely overwhelmed with shame, he hid his face in his hands.

Suddenly, a pair of soft arms stole around his neck, a childish, tear-wet cheek was pressed close to his, and a sweet voice whispered, tenderly: "Dear, I'm sorry! I'm so sorry I can't live another minute unless you tell me you forgive me!"

"Am I really a loafer?" asked Harlan, half an hour later.

"Indeed you're not," answered Dorothy, her trustful eyes looking straight into his; "you're absolutely the most adorable boy in the whole world, and it's me that knows it!"

"As long as you know it," returned Harlan, seriously, "I don't care a hang what other people think."

"Now, tell me," continued Dorothy, "how near are we to being broke?"

Obediently, Harlan turned his pockets inside out and piled his worldly wealth on the table.

"Three hundred and seventy-four dollars and sixteen cents," she said, when she had finished counting. "Why, we're almost rich, and a little while ago you tried to make me think we were poor!"

"It's all I have, Dorothy—every blooming cent, except one dollar in the savings bank. Sort of a nest egg I had left," he explained.

"Wait a minute," she said, reaching down into her collar and drawing up a loop of worn ribbon. "Straight front corset," she observed, flushing, "makes a nice pocket for almost everything." She drew up a chamois-skin bag, of an unprepossessing mouse colour, and emptied out a roll of bills. "Two hundred and twelve dollars," she said, proudly, "and eighty-three cents and four postage stamps in my purse.

"I saved it," she continued, hastily, "for an emergency, and I wanted some silk stockings and a French embroidered corset and some handmade lingerie worse than you can ever know. Wasn't I a brave, heroic, noble woman?"

"Indeed you were," he cried, "but, Dorothy, you know I can't touch your money!"

"Why not?" she demanded.

"Because—because—because it isn't right. Do you think I'm cad enough to live on a woman's earnings?"

"Harlan," said Dorothy, kindly, "don't be a fool. You'll take my whole heart and soul and life—all that I have been and all that I'm going to be—and be glad to get it, and now you're balking at ten cents that I happened to have in my stocking when I took the fatal step."

"Dear heart, don't. It's different—tremendously different. Can't you see that it is?"

"Do you mean that I'm not worth as much as two hundred and twelve dollars and eighty-three cents and four postage stamps?"

"Darling, you're worth more than all the rest of the world put together. Don't talk to me like that. But I can't touch your money, truly, dear, I can't; so don't ask me."

"Idiot," cried Dorothy, with tears raining down her face, "don't you know I'd go with you if you had to grind an organ in the street, and collect the money for you in a tin cup till we got enough for a monkey? What kind of a dinky little silver-plated wedding present do you think I am, anyway? You——"

The rest of it was sobbed out, incoherently enough, on his hitherto immaculate shirt-front. "You don't mind," she whispered, "if I cry down your neck, do you?"

"If you're going to cry," he answered, his voice trembling, "this is the one place for you to do it, but I don't want you to cry."

"I won't, then," she said, wiping her eyes on a wet and crumpled handkerchief. In a time astonishingly brief to one hitherto unfamiliar with the lachrymal function, her sobs had ceased.

"You've made me cry nearly a quart since morning," she went on, with assumed severity, "and I hope you'll behave so well from now on that I'll never have to do it again. Look here."

She led him to the window, where a pair of robins were building a nest in the boughs of a maple close by. "Do you see those birds?" she demanded, pointing at them with a dimpled, rosy forefinger.

"Yes, what of it?"

"Well, they're married, aren't they?"

"I hope they are," laughed Harlan, "or at least engaged."

"Who's bringing the straw and feathers for the nest?" she asked.

"Both, apparently," he replied, unwillingly.

"Why isn't she rocking herself on a bough, and keeping her nails nice, and fixing her feathers in the latest style, or perhaps going off to some fool bird club while he builds the nest by himself?"

"Don't know."

"Nor anybody else," she continued, with much satisfaction. "Now, if she happened to have two hundred and twelve feathers, of the proper size and shape to go into that nest, do you suppose he'd refuse to touch them, and make her cry because she brought them to him?"

"Probably he wouldn't," admitted Harlan.

There was a long silence, then Dorothy edged up closer to him. "Do you suppose," she queried, "that Mr. Robin thinks more of his wife than you do of yours?"

"Indeed he doesn't!"

"And still, he's letting her help him."

"But——"

"Now, listen, Harlan. We've got a house, with more than enough furniture to make it comfortable, though it's not the kind of furniture either of us particularly like. Instead of buying a typewriter, we'll rent one for three or four dollars a month until we have enough money to buy one. And I'm going to have a cow and some chickens and a garden, and I'm going to sell milk and butter and cream and fresh eggs and vegetables and chickens and fruit to the sanitarium, and——"

"The sanitarium people must have plenty of those things."

"But not the kind I'm going to raise, nor put up as I'm going to put it up, and we'll be raising most of our own living besides. You can write when you feel like it, and be helping me when you don't feel like it, and before we know it, we'll be rich. Oh, Harlan, I feel like Eve all alone in the Garden with Adam!"

The prospect fired his imagination, for, in common with most men, a chicken-ranch had appealed strongly to Harlan ever since he could remember.

"Well," he began, slowly, in the tone which was always a signal of surrender.

"Won't it be lovely," she cried ecstatically, "to have our own bossy cow mooing in the barn, and our own chickens for Sunday dinner, and our own milk, and butter, and cream? And I'll drive the vegetable waggon and you can take the things in——"

"I guess not," interrupted Harlan, firmly. "If you're going to do that sort of thing, you'll have people to do the work when I can't help you. The idea of my wife driving a vegetable cart!"

"All right," answered Dorothy, submissively, wise enough to let small points settle themselves and have her own way in things that really mattered. "I've not forgotten that I promised to obey you."

A gratified smile spread over Harlan's smooth, boyish face, and, half-fearfully, she reached into her sleeve for a handkerchief which she had hitherto carefully concealed.

"That's not all," she smiled. "Look!"

"Twenty-three dollars," he said. "Why, where did you get that?"

"It was in my dresser. There was a false bottom in one of the small drawers, and I took it out and found this."

"What in—" began Harlan.

"It's a present to us from Uncle Ebeneezer," she cried, her eyes sparkling and her face aglow. "It's for a coop and chickens," she continued, executing an intricate dance step. "Oh, Harlan, aren't you awfully glad we came?"

Seeing her pleasure he could not help being glad, but afterward, when he was alone, he began to wonder whether they had not inadvertently moved into a bank.

"Might be worse places," he reflected, "for the poor and deserving to move into. Diamonds and money—what next?"

# V

## Mrs. Smithers

The chickens were clucking peacefully in their corner of Uncle Ebeneezer's dooryard, and the newly acquired bossy cow mooed unhappily in her improvised stable. Harlan had christened the cow "Maud" because she insisted upon going into the garden, and though Dorothy had vigorously protested against putting Tennyson to such base uses, the name still held, out of sheer appropriateness.

Harlan was engaged in that pleasant pastime known as "pottering." The instinct to drive nails, put up shelves, and to improve generally his local habitation is as firmly seated in the masculine nature as housewifely characteristics are ingrained in the feminine soul. Never before having had a home of his own, Harlan was enjoying it to the full.

Early hours had been the rule at the Jack-o'-Lantern ever since the feathered sultan with his tribe of voluble wives had taken up his abode on the hilltop. Indeed, as Harlan said, they were obliged to sleep when the chickens did—if they slept at all. So it was not yet seven one morning when Dorothy went in from the chicken coop, singing softly to herself, and intent upon the particular hammer her husband wanted, never expecting to find Her in the kitchen.

"I—I beg your pardon?" she stammered, inquiringly.

A gaunt, aged, and preternaturally solemn female, swathed in crape, bent slightly forward in her chair, without making an effort to rise, and reached forth a black-gloved hand tightly grasping a letter, which was tremulously addressed to "Mrs. J. H. Carr."

"My dear Madam," Dorothy read.

"The multitudinous duties in connection with the practice of my profession have unfortunately prevented me, until the present hour, from interviewing Mrs. Sarah Smithers in regard to your requirements. While she is naturally unwilling to commit herself entirely without a more definite idea of what is expected of her, she is none the less kindly disposed. May I hope, my dear madam, that at the first opportunity you will apprise me of ensuing events in this connection, and that in any event I may still faithfully serve you?

"With kindest personal remembrances and my polite salutations to the distinguished author whose wife you have the honour to be, I am, my dear madam,

"Yr. most respectful and obedient servant,

"Jeremiah Bradford.

"Oh," said Dorothy, "you're Sarah. I had almost given you up."

"Begging your parding, Miss," rejoined Mrs. Smithers in a chilly tone of reproof, "but I take it it's better for us to begin callin' each other by our proper names. If we should get friendly, there'd be ample time to change. Your uncle, God rest 'is soul, allers called me 'Mis' Smithers.'"

Somewhat startled at first, Mrs. Carr quickly recovered her equanimity. "Very well, Mrs. Smithers," she returned, lightly, reflecting that when in Rome one must follow Roman customs; "Do you understand all branches of general housework?"

"If I didn't, I wouldn't be makin' no attempts in that direction," replied Mrs. Smithers, harshly. "I doesn't allow nobody to do wot I does no better than wot I does it."

Dorothy smiled, for this was distinctly encouraging, from at least one point of view.

"You wear a cap, I suppose?"

"Yes, mum, for dustin'. When I goes out I puts on my bonnet."

"Can you do plain cooking?" inquired Dorothy, hastily, perceiving that she was treading upon dangerous ground.

"Yes, mum. The more plain it is the better all around. Your uncle was never one to fill hisself with fancy dishes days and walk the floor with 'em nights, that's wot 'e wasn't."

"What wages do you have, Sa—Mrs. Smithers?"

"I worked for your uncle for a dollar and a half a week, bein' as we'd knowed each other so long, and on account of 'im bein' easy to get along with and never makin' no trouble, but I wouldn't work for no woman for less 'n two dollars."

"That is satisfactory to me," returned Dorothy, trying to be dignified. "I daresay we shall get on all right. Can you stay now?"

"If you've finished," said Mrs. Smithers, ignoring the question, "there's a few things I'd like to ask. 'Ow did you get that bruise on your face?"

"I—I ran into something," answered Dorothy, unwillingly, and taken quite by surprise.

"Wot was it," demanded Mrs. Smithers. "Your 'usband's fist?"

"No," replied Mrs. Carr, sternly, "it was a piece of furniture."

"I've never knowed furniture," observed Mrs. Smithers, doubtfully, "to get up and 'it people in the face wot wasn't doin' nothink to it. If you disturb a rockin'-chair at night w'en it's restin' quiet, you'll get your ankle 'it, but I've never knowed no furniture to 'it people under the eye unless it 'ad been threw, that's wot I ain't.

"I mind me of my youngest sister," Mrs. Smithers went on, her keen eyes uncomfortably fixed upon Dorothy. "'Er 'usband was one of these 'ere masterful men, 'e was, same as wot yours is, and w'en 'er didn't please 'im, 'e 'd 'it 'er somethink orful. Many's the time I've gone there and found 'er with 'er poor face all cut up and the crockery broke bad. 'I dropped a cup' 'er'd say to me, 'and the pieces flew up and 'it me in the face.' 'Er face looked like a crazy quilt from 'aving dropped so many cups, and wunst, without thinkin' wot I might be doin' of, I gave 'er a chiny tea set for 'er Christmas present.

"Wen I went to see 'er again, the tea set was all broke and 'er 'ad court plaster all over 'er face. The pieces must 'ave flew more 'n common from the tea set, cause 'er 'usband's 'ed was laid open somethink frightful and they'd 'ad in the doctor to take a seam in it. From that time on I never 'eard of no more cups bein' dropped and 'er face looked quite human and peaceful like w'en 'e died. God rest 'is soul, 'e ain't a-breakin' no tea sets now by accident nor a-purpose neither. I was never one to interfere between man and wife, Miss Carr, but I want you to tell your 'usband that should 'e undertake to 'it me, 'e'll get a bucket of 'ot tea throwed in 'is face."

"It's not at all likely," answered Dorothy, biting her lip, "that such a thing will happen." She was swayed by two contradictory impulses—one to scream with laughter, the other to throw something at Mrs. Smithers.

"'E's been at peace now six months come Tuesday," continued Mrs. Smithers, "and on account of 'is 'avin' broke the tea set, I don't feel no call to wear mourning for 'im more 'n a year, though folks thinks as 'ow it brands me as 'eartless for takin' it off inside of two. Sakes alive, wot's that?" she cried, drawing her sable skirts more closely about her as a dark shadow darted across the kitchen.

"It's only the cat," answered Dorothy, reassuringly. "Come here, Claudius."

Mrs. Smithers repressed an exclamation of horror as Claudius, purring pleasantly, came out into the sunlight, brandishing his plumed tail, and sat down on the edge of Dorothy's skirt, blinking his green eyes at the intruder.

"'E's the very cat," said Mrs. Smithers, hoarsely, "wot your uncle killed the week afore 'e died!"

"Before who died?" asked Dorothy, a chill creeping into her blood.

"Your uncle," whispered Mrs. Smithers, her eyes still fixed upon Claudius Tiberius. "'E killed that very cat, 'e did, 'cause 'e couldn't never abide 'im, and now 'e's come back!"

"Nonsense!" cried Dorothy, trying to be severe. "If he killed the cat, it couldn't come back—you must know that."

"I don't know w'y not, Miss. Anyhow, 'e killed the cat, that's wot 'e did, and I saw 'is dead body, and even buried 'im, on account of your uncle not bein' able to abide cats, and 'ere 'e is. Somebody 's dug 'im up, and 'e 's come to life again, thinkin' to 'aunt your uncle, and your uncle 'as follered 'im, that's wot 'e 'as, and there bein' nobody 'ere to 'aunt but us, 'e's a 'auntin' us and a-doin' it 'ard."

"Mrs. Smithers," said Dorothy, rising, "I desire to hear no more of this nonsense. The cat happens to be somewhat similar to the dead one, that's all."

"Begging your parding, Miss, for askin', but did you bring that there cat with you from the city?"

Affecting not to hear, Dorothy went out, followed by Claudius Tiberius, who appeared anything but ghostly.

"I knowed it," muttered Mrs. Smithers, gloomily, to herself. "'E was 'ere w'en 'er come, and 'e's the same cat. 'E's come back to 'aunt us, that's wot 'e 'as!"

"Harlan," said Dorothy, half-way between smiles and tears, "she's come."

Harlan dropped his saw and took up his hammer. "Who's come?" he asked. "From your tone, it might be Mrs. Satan, or somebody else from the infernal regions."

"You're not far out of the way," rejoined Dorothy. "It's Sa—Mrs. Smithers."

"Oh, our maid of all work?"

"I don't know what she's made of," giggled Dorothy, hysterically. "She looks like a tombstone dressed in deep mourning, and carries with her the atmosphere of a graveyard. We have to call her 'Mrs. Smithers,' if we don't want her to call us by our first names, and she has two dollars a week. She says Claudius is a cat that uncle killed the week before he died, and she thinks you hit me and gave me this bruise on my cheek."

"The old lizard," said Harlan, indignantly. "She sha'n't stay!"

"Now don't be cross," interrupted Dorothy. "It's all in the family, for your uncle hit me, as you well know. Besides, we can't expect all the virtues for two dollars a week and I'm tired almost to death from trying to do the housework in this big house and take care of the chickens, too. We'll get on with her as best we can until we see a chance to do better."

"Wise little woman," responded Harlan, admiringly. "Can she milk the cow?"

"I don't know—I'll go in and ask her."

"Excuse me, Miss," began Mrs. Smithers, before Dorothy had a chance to speak, "but am I to 'ave my old rooms?"

"Which rooms were they?"

"These 'ere, back of the kitchen. My own settin' room and bedroom and kitchen and pantry and my own private door outside. Your uncle was allers a great hand for bein' private and insistin' on other folks keepin' private, that 's wot 'e was, but God rest 'is soul, it didn't do the poor old gent much good."

"Certainly," said Dorothy, "take your old rooms. And can you milk a cow?"

Mrs. Smithers sighed. "I ain't never 'ad it put on me, Miss," she said, with the air of a martyr trying to make himself comfortable up against the stake, "not as a regler thing, I ain't, but wotever I'm asked to do in the line of duty whiles I'm dwellin' in this sufferin' and dyin' world, I aims to do the best wot I can, w'ether it's milkin' a cow, drownin' kittens, or buryin' a cat wot can't stay buried."

"We have breakfast about half-past seven," went on Dorothy, quickly; "luncheon at noon and dinner at six."

"Wot at six?" demanded Mrs. Smithers, pricking up her ears.

"Dinner! Dinner at six."

"Lord preserve us," said Mrs. Smithers, half to herself. "Your uncle allers 'ad 'is dinner at one o'clock, sharp, and 'e wouldn't like it to 'ave such scandalous goin's on in 'is own 'ouse."

"You're working for me," Dorothy reminded her sharply, "and not for my uncle."

There was a long silence, during which Mrs. Smithers peered curiously at her young mistress over her steel-bowed spectacles. "I'm not so sure as you," she said. "On account of the cat 'avin come back from 'is grave, it wouldn't surprise me none to see your uncle settin' 'ere at any time in 'is shroud, and a-askin' to 'ave mush and milk for 'is supper, the which 'e was so powerful fond of that I was more 'n 'alf minded at the last minute to put some of it in 's coffin."

"Mrs. Smithers," said Dorothy, severely, "I do not want to hear any more about dead people, or resurrected cats, or anything of that nature. What's gone is gone, and there's no use in continually referring to it."

At this significant moment, Claudius Tiberius paraded somewhat ostentatiously through the kitchen and went outdoors.

"You see, Miss?" asked Mrs. Smithers, with ill-concealed satisfaction. "Wot's gone ain't always gone for long, that's wot it ain't."

Dorothy retreated, followed by a sepulchral laugh which grated on her nerves. "Upon my word, dear," she said to Harlan, "I don't know how we're going to stand having that woman in the house. She makes me feel as if I were an undertaker, a grave digger, and a cemetery, all rolled into one."

"You're too imaginative," said Harlan, tenderly, stroking her soft cheek. He had not yet seen Mrs. Smithers.

"Perhaps," Dorothy admitted, "when she gets that pyramid of crape off her head, she'll seem more nearly human. Do you suppose she expects to wear it in the house all the time?"

"Miss Carr!"

The gaunt black shadow appeared in the doorway of the kitchen and the high, harsh voice shrilled imperiously across the yard.

"I'm coming," answered Dorothy, submissively, for in the tone there was that which instinctively impels obedience. "What is it?" she asked, when she entered the kitchen.

"Nothink. I only wants to know wot it is you're layin' out to 'ave for your— luncheon, if that's wot you call it."

"Poached eggs on toast, last night's cold potatoes warmed over, hot biscuits, jam, and tea."

Mrs. Smithers's articulate response resembled a cluck more closely than anything else.

"You can make biscuits, can't you?" went on Dorothy, hastily.

"I 'ave," responded Mrs. Smithers, dryly. "Begging your parding, Miss, but is that there feller sawin' wood out by the chicken coop your 'usband?"

"The gentleman in the yard," said Dorothy, icily, "is Mr. Carr."

"Be n't you married to 'im?" cried Mrs. Smithers, dropping a fork. "I understood as 'ow you was, else I wouldn't 'ave come. I was never one to——"

"I most assuredly *am* married to him," answered Dorothy, with due emphasis on the verb.

"Oh! 'E's the build of my youngest sister's poor dead 'usband; the one wot broke the tea set wot I give 'er over 'er poor 'ed. 'E can 'it powerful 'ard, can't 'e?"

Quite beyond speech, Dorothy went outdoors again, her head held high and a dangerous light in her eyes. To-morrow, or next week at the latest, should witness the forced departure of Mrs. Smithers. Mrs. Carr realised that the woman did not intend to be impertinent, and that the social forms of Judson Centre were not those of New York. Still, some things were unbearable.

The luncheon that was set before them, however, went far toward atonement. With the best intentions in the world, Dorothy's cooking nearly always went wide of the mark, and Harlan welcomed the change with unmistakable pleasure.

"I say, Dorothy," he whispered, as they rose from the table; "get on with her if you can. Anybody who can make such biscuits as these will go out of the house only over my dead body."

The latter part of the speech was unfortunate. "My surroundings are so extremely cheerful," remarked Dorothy, "that I've decided to spend the afternoon in the library reading Poe. I've always wanted to do it and I don't believe I'll ever feel any creepier than I do this blessed minute."

In spite of his laughing protest, she went into the library, locked the door, and curled up in Uncle Ebeneezer's easy chair with a well-thumbed volume of Poe, finding a two-dollar bill used in one place as a book mark. She read for some time, then took down another book, which opened of itself at "The Gold Bug."

The pages were thickly strewn with marginal comments in the fine, small, shaky hand she had learned to associate with Uncle Ebeneezer. The paragraph about the skull, in the tree above the treasure, had evidently filled the last reader with unprecedented admiration, for on the margin was written twice, in ink: "A very, very pretty idea."

She laughed aloud, for her thoughts since morning had been persistently directed toward things not of this world. "I'm glad I'm not superstitious," she thought, then jumped almost out of her chair at the sound of an ominous crash in the kitchen.

"I won't go," she thought, settling back into her place. "I'll let that old monument alone just as much as I can."

Upon the whole, it was just as well, for the "old monument" was on her bony knees, with her head and shoulders quite lost in the secret depths of the kitchen range. "I wonder," she was muttering, "where 'e could 'ave put it. It would 'ave been just like that old skinflint to 'ave 'id it in the stove!"

# VI

# The Coming of Elaine

There is no state of mental wretchedness akin to that which precedes the writing of a book. Harlan was moody and despairing, chiefly because he could not understand what it all meant. Something hung over him like a black cloud, completely obscuring his usual sunny cheerfulness.

He burned with the desire to achieve, yet from the depths of his soul came only emptiness. Vague, purposeless aspirations, like disembodied spirits, haunted him by night and by day. Before his inner vision came unfamiliar scenes, detached fragments of conversation, the atmosphere, the feeling of an old romance, then, by a swift change, darkness from which there seemed no possible escape.

A woman with golden hair, mounted upon a white horse, gay with scarlet and silver trappings—surely her name was Elaine? And thecompany of gallant knights who followed her as she set forth upon her quest—who were they, and from whence did they hail? The fool of the court, with his bauble and his cracked, meaningless laughter, danced in and out of the picture with impish glee. Behind it all was the sunset, such a sunset as was never seen on land or sea. Ribbons of splendid colour streamed from the horizon to the zenith and set the shields of the knights aglow with shimmering flame. Clashing cymbals sounded from afar, then, clear and high, a bugle call, the winding silvery notes growing fainter and fainter till they were lost in the purple silence of the hills. Elaine turned, smiling—was not her name Elaine? And then——

Darkness fell and the picture was utterly wiped out. Harlan turned away with a sigh.

To take the dead, dry bones of words, the tiny black things that march in set spaces across the page; to set each where it inevitably belongs—truly, it seems simple enough. But from the vast range of our written speech to select those which fittingly clothe the thought is quite another matter, and presupposes the thought. Even then, by necessity, the outcome is uncertain.

Within the mind of the writer, the Book lives and breathes; a child of the brain, yearning for birth. At a white heat, after long waiting, the words come—merely a commentary, an index, a marginal note of that within. Reading afterward the written words, the fine invisible links, the colour and the music, are treacherously supplied by the imagination, which is at once the best friend and the worst enemy. How is one to know that only a small part of it has been written, that the best of it, far past writing, lingers still unborn?

Long afterward, when the original picture has faded as though it had never been, one may read his printed work, and wonder, in abject self-abasement, by what miracle it was ever printed. He has trusted to some unknown psychology which strongly savours of the Black Art to reproduce in the minds of his readers the picture which was in his, and from which these fragmentary, marginal notes were traced. Only the words, the dead, meaningless words, stripped of all the fancy which once made them fair, to make for the thousands the wild, delirious bliss that the writer knew! To write with the tears falling upon the page, and afterward to read, in some particularly poignant and searching review, that "the book fails to convince!" Happy is he whose written pages reproduce but faintly the glow from whence they came. For "whoso with blood and tears would dig Art out of his soul, may lavish his golden prime in pursuit of emptiness, or, striking treasure, find only fairy gold, so that when his eyes are purged of the spell of morning, he sees his hands are full of withered leaves."

A meadow-lark, rising from a distant field, dropped golden notes into the still, sunlit air, then vanished into the blue spaces beyond. A bough of apple bloom, its starry petals anchored only by invisible cobwebs, softly shook white fragrance into the grass. Then, like a vision straight from the golden city with the walls of pearl, came Elaine, the beautiful, her blue eyes laughing, and her scarlet lips parted in a smile.

Harlan's heart sang within him. His trembling hands grasped feverishly at the sheaf of copy-paper which had waited for this, week in and week out. The pencil was ready to his hand, and the words fairly wrote themselves:

*It came to pass that when the year was at the Spring, the Lady Elaine fared forth upon the Heart's Quest. She was mounted upon a snowy palfrey, whose trappings of scarlet and silver gleamed brightly in the sun. Her gown was of white satin, wondrously embroidered in fine gold thread, which was no less gold than her hair, falling in unchecked splendour about her.*

*Blue as sapphires were the eyes of Elaine, and her fair cheek was like that of an apple-blossom. Set like a rose upon pearl was the dewy, fragrant sweetness of her mouth, and her breath was like that of the rose itself. Her hands—but how shall I write of the flower-like hands of Elaine? They—*

The door-bell pealed portentously through the house, echoing and re-echoing through the empty rooms. No answer. Presently it rang again, insistently, and Elaine, with her snowy palfrey, whisked suddenly out of sight.

Gone, except for these few lines! Harlan stifled a groan and the bell rang once more.

Heavens! Where was Dorothy? Where was Mrs. Smithers? Was there no one in the house but himself? Apparently not, for the bell rang determinedly, and with military precision.

"March, march, forward march!" grumbled Harlan, as he ran downstairs, the one-two, one-two-three being registered meanwhile on the bell-wire.

It was not a pleasant person who violently wrenched the door open, but in spite of his annoyance, Harlan could not be discourteous to a lady. She was tall, and slender, and pale, with blue eyes and yellow hair, and so very fragile that it seemed as though a passing zephyr might almost blow her away.

"How do you do," she said, wearily. "I thought you were never coming."

"I was busy," said Harlan, in extenuation. "Will you come in?" She was evidently a friend of Dorothy's, and, as such, demanded proper consideration.

The invitation was needless, however, for even as he spoke, she brushed past him, and went into the parlour. "I'm so tired," she breathed. "I walked up that long hill."

"You shouldn't have done it," returned Harlan, standing first on one foot and then on the other. "Couldn't you find the stage?"

"I didn't look for it. I never had any ambition to go on the stage," she concluded, with a faint smile. "Where is Uncle Ebeneezer?"

"No friend of Dorothy's," thought Harlan, shifting to the other foot. "Uncle Ebeneezer," he said, clearing his throat, "is at peace."

"What do you mean?" demanded the girl, sinking into one of the haircloth chairs. "Where is Uncle Ebeneezer?"

"Uncle Ebeneezer is dead," explained Harlan, somewhat tartly. Then, as he remembered the utter ruin of his work, he added, viciously, "never having known him intimately, I can't say just where he is."

She leaned back in her chair, her face as white as death. Harlan thought she had fainted, when she relieved his mind by bursting into tears. He was more familiar with salt water, but, none the less, the situation was awkward.

There were no signs of Dorothy, so Harlan, in an effort to be consoling, took the visitor's cold hands in his. "Don't," he said, kindly; "cheer up. You are among friends."

"I have no friends," she answered, between sobs. "I lost the last when my dear mother died. She made me promise, during her last illness, that if anything happened to her, I would come to Uncle Ebeneezer. She said she had never imposed upon him and that he would gladly take care of me, for her sake. I was

ill a long, long time, but as soon as I was able to, I came, and now—and now—
—"

"Don't," said Harlan, again, awkwardly patting her hands, and deeply touched by the girl's distress. "We are your friends. You can stay here just as well as not. I am married and——"

Upon his back, Harlan felt eyes. He turned quickly, and saw Dorothy standing in the door—quite a new Dorothy, indeed; very tall, and stately, and pale.

Through sheer nervousness, Mr. Carr laughed—an unfortunate, high-pitched laugh with no mirth in it. "Let me present my wife," he said, sobering suddenly. "Mrs. Carr, Miss——"

Here he coughed, and the guest, rising, filled the pause. "I am Elaine St. Clair," she explained, offering a white, tremulous hand which Dorothy did not seem to see. "It is very good of your husband to ask me to stay with you."

"Very," replied Dorothy, in a tone altogether new to her husband. "He is always doing lovely things for people. And now, Harlan, if you will show Miss St. Clair to her room, I will speak with Mrs. Smithers about luncheon, which should be nearly ready by this time."

"Thunder," said Harlan to himself, as Dorothy withdrew. "What in the devil do I know about 'her room'? Have you ever been here before?" he inquired of the guest.

"Never in my life," answered Miss St. Clair, wiping her eyes.

"Well," replied Harlan, confusedly, "just go on upstairs, then, and help yourself. There are plenty of rooms, and cribs to burn in every blamed one of 'em," he added, savagely, remembering the look in Dorothy's eyes.

"Thank you," said Miss St. Clair, diffidently; "it is very kind of you to let me choose. Can some one bring my trunk up this afternoon?"

"I'll attend to it," replied her host, brusquely.

She trailed noiselessly upstairs, carrying her heavy suit case, and Harlan, not altogether happy at the prospect, went in search of Dorothy. At the kitchen door he paused, hearing voices within.

"They've usually et by themselves," Mrs. Smithers was saying. "Is this a new one, or a friend of yours?"

The sentence was utterly without meaning, either to Harlan or Dorothy, but the answer was given, as quick as a flash. "A friend, Mrs. Smithers—a very dear old friend of Mr. Carr's."

"'Mr. Carr's,'" repeated Harlan, miserably, tiptoeing away to the library, where he sat down and wiped his forehead. "'A very dear old friend.'" Disconnectedly, and with pronounced emphasis, Harlan mentioned the place which is said to be paved with good intentions.

The clock struck twelve, and it was just eleven when he had begun on *The Quest of the Lady Elaine*. "'One crowded hour of glorious life is worth'—what idiot said it was worth anything?" groaned Harlan, inwardly. "Anyway, I've had the crowded hour. 'Better fifty years of Europe than a cycle of Cathay'"— the line sang itself into his consciousness. "Europe be everlastingly condemned," he muttered. "Oh, how my head aches!"

He leaned back in his chair, wondering where "Cathay" might be. It sounded like a nice, quiet place, with no "dear old friends" in it—a peaceful spot where people could write books if they wanted to. "Just why," he asked himself more than once, "was I inspired to grab the shaky paw of that human sponge? 'Tears, idle tears, I know not what they mean'—oh, the devil! She must have a volume of Tennyson in her grip, and it's soaking through!"

Mrs. Smithers came out into the hall, more sepulchral and grim-visaged than ever, and rang the bell for luncheon. To Harlan's fevered fancy, it sounded like a sexton tolling a bell for a funeral. Miss St. Clair, with the traces of tears practically removed, floated gracefully downstairs, and Harlan, coming out of the library with the furtive step of a wild beast from its lair, met her inopportunely at the foot of the stairs.

She smiled at him in a timid, but friendly fashion, and at the precise moment, Dorothy appeared in the dining-room door.

"Harlan, dear," she said, in her sweetest tones, "will you give our guest your arm and escort her out to luncheon? I have it all ready!"

Miss St. Clair clutched timidly at Harlan's rigid coat sleeve, wondering what strange custom of the house would be evident next, and the fog was thick before Mr. Carr's eyes, when he took his accustomed seat at the head of the table. As a sign of devotion, he tried to step on Dorothy's foot under the table, after a pleasing habit of their courtship in the New York boarding-house, but he succeeded only in drawing an unconscious "ouch" and a vivid blush from Miss St. Clair, by which he impressed Dorothy more deeply than he could have hoped to do otherwise.

"Have you come far, Miss St. Clair?" asked Dorothy, conventionally.

"From New York," answered the guest, taking a plate of fried chicken from Harlan's shaky hand.

"I know," said Dorothy sweetly. "We come from New York, too." Then she took a bold, daring plunge. "I have often heard my husband speak of you."

"Of me, Mrs. Carr? Surely not! It must have been some other Elaine."

"Perhaps," smiled Dorothy, shrugging her shoulders. "No doubt I am mistaken, but you may have heard of me?"

"Indeed I haven't," Elaine assured her. "I never heard of you in my life before. Why should I?" A sudden and earnest crow under the window behind her startled her so that she dropped her knife. Harlan stooped for it at the same time she did and their heads bumped together smartly.

"Our gentleman chicken," went on Dorothy, tactfully. "We call him 'Abdul Hamid.' You know the masculine nature is instinctively polygamous."

Harlan cackled mirthlessly, wondering, subconsciously, how Abdul Hamid could have escaped from the coop. After that there was silence, save as Dorothy, in her most hospitable manner, occasionally urged the guest to have more of something. Throughout luncheon, she never once spoke to Harlan, nor took so much as a single glance at his red, unhappy face. Even his ears were scarlet, and the delicious fried chicken which he was eating might have been a section of rag carpet, for all he knew to the contrary.

"And now, Miss St. Clair," said Dorothy, kindly, as they rose from the table, "I am sure you will wish to lie down and rest after your long journey. Which room did you choose?"

"I looked at all of them," responded Elaine, touched to the heart by this unexpected kindness from strangers, "and finally chose the suite in the south wing. It's a nice large room, with such a darling little sitting-room attached, and such a dear work basket."

Harlan nearly burst, for the description was of Dorothy's own particular sanctum.

"Yes," said Mrs. Carr, very quietly; "I thought my husband would choose that room for you—dear Harlan is always so thoughtful! I will go up with you and take out a few of my things which have been unfortunately left there."

Shortly afterward, Mr. Carr also climbed the stairs, his head swimming and his knees knocking together. Nervously, he turned over the few pages of his manuscript, then, hearing Dorothy coming, grabbed it and fled like a thief to the library on the first floor. In his panic he bolted the doors and windows of Uncle Ebeneezer's former retreat. It was unnecessary, however, for no one came near him.

Throughout the long, sweet Spring afternoon, Miss St. Clair slept the dreamless sleep of utter exhaustion, Harlan worked fruitlessly at *The Quest of Lady Elaine*, and Dorothy busied herself about her household tasks, singing with forced cheerfulness whenever she was within hearing of the library.

"I'll explain" thought Harlan, wretchedly. But after all what was there to explain, except that he had never seen Miss St. Clair before, never in all his life heard of her, never knew there was such a person, or had never met anybody who knew anything about her? "Besides," he continued to himself "even then, what excuse have I got for stroking a strange woman's hand and telling her I'm married?"

As the afternoon wore on, he decided that it would be policy to ignore the whole matter. It was an unfortunate misunderstanding all around, which could not be cleared away by speech, unless Dorothy should ask him about it—which he was very certain she would not do. "She ought to trust me," he said to himself, resentfully, forgetting the absolute openness of thought and deed upon which a woman's trust is founded. "I'll read her the book to-night," he thought, happily, "and that will please her."

But it was fated not to. After dinner, which was much the same as luncheon, as far as conversation was concerned, Harlan invited Dorothy to come into the library.

She followed him, obediently enough, and he closed the door.

"Dearest," he began, with a grin which was meant to be cheerful and was merely ridiculous, "I've begun the book—I actually have! I've been working on it all day. Just listen!"

Hurriedly possessing himself of the manuscript, he read it in an unnatural voice, down to the flower-like hands.

"I don't see how you can say that, Harlan," interrupted Dorothy, coolly critical; "I particularly noticed her hands and they're not nice at all. They're red and rough and nearly the size of a policeman's."

"Whose hands?" demanded Harlan, in genuine astonishment.

"Why, Elaine's—Miss St. Clair's. If you're going to do a book about her, you might at least try to make it truthful."

Mrs. Carr went out, closing the door carefully, but firmly. Then, for the first time, the whole wretched situation dawned upon the young and aspiring author.

# VII

## An Uninvited Guest

Dorothy sat alone in her room, facing the first heartache of her married life. She repeatedly told herself that she was not jealous; that the primitive, unlovely emotion was far beneath such as she. But if Harlan had only told her, instead of leaving her to find out in this miserable way! It had never entered her head that the clear-eyed, clean-minded boy whom she had married, could have anything even remotely resembling a past, and here it was in her own house! Moreover, it had inspired a book, and she herself had been unable to get him to work at all.

Just why women should be concerned in regard to old loves has never been wholly clear. One might as well fancy a clean slate, freshly and elaborately dedicated to noble composition, being bothered by the addition and subtraction which was once done upon its surface.

With her own eyes she had seen Miss St. Clair weeping, while Harlan held her hands and explained that he was married. Undoubtedly Miss St. Clair accounted for various metropolitan delays and absences which she had joyously forgiven on the score of Harlan's "work." Bitterest of all was the thought that she must endure it—that the long years ahead of her offered no escape, no remedy, except the ignoble, painful one which she would not for a moment consider.

A sudden flash of resentment stiffened her backbone, metaphorically speaking. In spite of Miss St. Clair, Harlan had married her, and it was Miss St. Clair who was weeping over the event, not Harlan. She had seen that the visitor made Harlan unhappy—very well, she would generously throw them together and make him painfully weary of her, for Love's certain destroyer is Satiety. Deep in Dorothy's consciousness was the abiding satisfaction that she had never once, as she put it to herself, "chased him." Never a note, never a telephone call, never a question as to his coming and going appeared now to trouble her. The ancient, primeval relation of the Seeker and the Sought had not for a single moment been altered through her.

Meanwhile, Elaine had settled down peacefully enough. Having been regaled since infancy with tales of Uncle Ebeneezer's generous hospitality, it seemed only fitting and proper that his relatives should make her welcome, even though

Elaine's mother had been only a second cousin of Mrs. Judson's. Elaine had been deeply touched by Harlan's solicitude and Dorothy's kindness, seeing in it nothing more than the manifestation of a beautiful spirit toward one who was helpless and ill.

A modest wardrobe and a few hundred dollars, saved from the wreck of her mother's estate, and the household furniture in storage, represented Elaine's worldly goods. As too often happens in a material world, she had been trained to do nothing but sing a little, play a little, and paint unspeakably. She planned, vaguely, to stay where she was during the Summer, and in the Autumn, when she had quite recovered her former strength, to take her money and learn some method of self-support.

Just now she was resting. A late breakfast, a walk through the country, a light luncheon, and a long nap accounted for Elaine's day until dinner-time. After dinner, for an hour, she exchanged commonplaces with the Carrs, then retired to her own room with a book from Uncle Ebeneezer's library. Even Dorothy was forced to admit that she made very little trouble.

The train rumbled into the station—the very same train which had brought the Serpent into Paradise. Dorothy smiled a little at the idea of a snake travelling on a train unless it belonged to a circus, and wiped her eyes. Having mapped out her line of conduct, the rest was simple enough—to abide by it even to the smallest details, and patiently await results.

When she went downstairs again she was outwardly quite herself, but altogether unprepared for the surprise that awaited her in the parlour.

"Hello," cried a masculine voice, cheerily, as she entered the room. "I've never seen you before, have I?"

"Not that I know of," replied Dorothy, startled, but not in the least afraid.

The young man who rose to greet her was not at all unpleasant to look upon. He was taller than Harlan, smooth-shaven, had nice brown eyes, and a mop of curly brown hair which evidently annoyed him. Moreover, he was laughing, as much from sheer joy of living as anything else.

"Which side of the house are you a relative of?" he asked.

"The inside," returned Dorothy. "I keep house here."

"You don't say so! What's become of Sally? Uncle shoo her off the lot?"

"I don't know what you're talking about," answered Dorothy, with a fruitless effort to appear matronly and dignified. "If by 'uncle' you mean Uncle Ebeneezer, he's dead."

"You don't tell me! Reaped at last, after all this delay! Then how did you come here?"

"By train," responded Dorothy, enjoying the situation to the utmost. "Uncle Ebeneezer left the house and furniture to my husband."

The young man sank into a chair and wiped the traces of deep emotion from his ruddy face. "Hully Gee!" he said, when he recovered speech. "I suppose that's French for 'Dick, chase yourself.'"

"Perhaps not," suggested Mrs. Carr, strangely loath to have this breezy individual take his departure. "You might tell me who you are; don't you think so?"

"Not a bad notion at all. I'm the Dick of the firm of 'Tom, Dick, and Harry,' you've doubtless heard about from your childhood. My other name is Chester, but few know it. I'm merely 'Dick' to everybody, yourself included, I trust," he added with an elaborate bow. "If you will sit down, and make yourself comfortable, I will now unfold to you the sad story of my life.

"I was born of poor but honest parents about twenty-three years ago, according to the last official census. They brought me up until I reached the ripe age of twelve, then got tired of their job and went to heaven. Since then I've brought myself up. I've just taught a college all it can learn from me, and been put out. Prexy confided to me that I wasn't going to graduate, so I shook the classic dust from my weary feet and fled hither as to a harbour of refuge. I've always spent my Summers with Uncle Ebeneezer, because it was cheap for me and good for him, but I can't undertake to follow him up this Summer, not knowing exactly where he is, and not caring for a warm climate anyway."

Inexpressibly shocked, Dorothy looked up to the portrait over the mantel half fearfully, but there was no change in the stern, malicious old face.

"You're afraid of him, aren't you?" asked Dick, with a hearty laugh.

"I always have been," admitted Dorothy. "He scared me the first time we came here—it was at night, and raining."

"I've known him to scare people in broad daylight, and they weren't always women either. He used to be a pleasant old codger, but he got over it, and after he learned to swear readily, he was a pretty tough party to buck up against. It took nerve to stay here when uncle was in a bad mood, but most people have more nerve than they think they have. You haven't told me your name yet."

"Mrs. Carr—Dorothy Carr."

"Pretty name," remarked Dick, with evident admiration. "If you don't mind, I'll call you 'Dorothy' till the train goes back. It will be something for me to remember in the desert waste of my empty years to come."

A friendly, hospitable impulse seized Mrs. Carr. "Why should you go?" she inquired, smiling. "If you've been in the habit of spending your Summers here, you needn't change on our account. We'd be glad to have you, I'm sure. A dear old friend of my husband's is already here."

"Fine or superfine?"

"Superfine," returned Dorothy, feeling very much as though the clock had been turned back twenty years or more and she was at a children's party again.

"You can bet your sweet life I'll stay," said Dick, "and if I bother you at any time, just say so and I'll skate out, with no hard feelings on either side. You may need me when the rest of the bunch gets here."

"The rest of—oh Harlan, come here a minute!"

She had caught him as he was going into the library with his work, thinking that a change of environment might possibly produce an acceptable change in the current of his thoughts.

"Dick," said Dorothy, when Harlan came to the door, "this is my husband. Mr. Chester, Mr. Carr."

For days Harlan had not seen Dorothy with such rosy cheeks, such dancing eyes, nor half as many dimples. Bewildered, and not altogether pleased, he awkwardly extended his hand to Mr. Chester, with a conventional "how do you do?"

Dick wrung the offered hand in a mighty grip which made Harlan wince. "I congratulate you, Mr. Carr," he said gallantly, "upon possessing the fairest ornament of her sex. Guess this letter is for you, isn't it? I found it in the post-office while the keeper was out, and just took it. If it doesn't belong here, I'll skip back with it."

"Thanks," murmured Harlan, rubbing the injured hand with the other. "I—where did you come from?"

"The station," explained Dick, pleasantly. "I never trace myself back of where I was last seen."

"He's going to stay with us, Harlan," put in Dorothy, wickedly, "so you mustn't let us keep you away from your work. Come along, Dick, and I'll show you our cow."

They went out, followed by a long, low whistle of astonishment from Harlan which Dorothy's acute ears did not miss. Presently Mr. Carr retreated into the library, and locked the door, but he did not work. The book was at a deadlock, half a paragraph beyond "the flower-like hands of Elaine," of which, indeed, the author had confessed his inability to write.

"Dick," thought Harlan. "Mr. Chester. A young giant with a grip like an octopus. 'The fairest ornament of her sex.' Never, never heard of him before. Some old flame of Dorothy's, who has discovered her whereabouts and brazenly followed her, even on her honeymoon."

And he, Harlan, was absolutely prevented from speaking of it by an unhappy chain of circumstances which put him in a false light! For the first time he fully perceived how a single thoughtless action may bind all one's future existence.

"Just because I stroked the hand of a distressed damsel," muttered Harlan, "and told her I was married, I've got to sit and see a procession of my wife's old lovers marking time here all Summer!" In his fevered fancy, he already saw the Jack-o'-Lantern surrounded by Mrs. Carr's former admirers, heard them call her "Dorothy," and realised that there was not a single thing he could do.

"Unless, of course," he added, mentally, "it gets too bad, and I have an excuse to order 'em out. And then, probably, Dorothy will tell Elaine to take her dolls and go home, and the poor thing's got nowhere to go—nowhere in the wide world.

"How would Dorothy like to be a lonely orphan, with no husband, no friends, and no job? She wouldn't like it much, but women never have any sympathy for each other, nor for their husbands, either. I'd give twenty dollars this minute not to have stroked Elaine's hand, and fifty not to have had Dorothy see it, but there's no use in crying over spilt milk nor in regretting hands that have already been stroked."

In search of diversion, he opened his letter, which was in answer to the one he had written some little time ago, inquiring minutely, of an acquaintance who was supposed to be successful, just what the prospects were for a beginner in the literary craft.

"Dear Carr," the letter read. "Sorry not to have answered before, but I've been away and things got mixed up. Wouldn't advise anybody but an enemy to take up writing as a steady job, but if you feel the call, go in and win. You can make all the way from eight dollars a year, which was what I made when I first struck out, up to five thousand, which was what I averaged last year. I've always envied you fellows who could turn in your stuff and get paid for it the following Tuesday. In my line, you work like the devil this year for what you're going to get next, and live on the year after.

"However, if you're bitten with it, there's no cure. You'll see magazine articles in stones and books in running brooks all the rest of your life. When you get your book done, I'll trot you around to my publisher, who enjoys the proud distinction of being an honest one, and if he likes your stuff, he'll take it, and if he doesn't, he'll turn you down so pleasantly that you'll feel as though he'd made you a present of something. If you think you've got genius, forget it, and remember that nothing takes the place of hard work. And, besides, it's a pretty blamed poor book that can't get itself printed these days.

"Yours as usual,

"C. J."

The communication was probably intended as encouragement, but the effect was depressing, and at the end of an hour, Harlan had written only two lines more in his book, neither of which pleased him.

Meanwhile, Dick was renewing his old acquaintance with Mrs. Smithers, much to that lady's pleasure, though she characteristically endeavoured to conceal it. She belonged to a pious sect which held all mirth to be ungodly.

"Sally," Dick was saying, "I've dreamed of your biscuits night and day since I ate the last one. Are we going to have 'em for lunch?"

"No biscuits in this house to-day," grumbled the deity of the kitchen, in an attempt to be properly stern, "and as I've told you more than once, my name ain't 'Sally.' It's Mis' Smithers, that's wot it is, and I'll thank you to call me by it."

"Between those who love," continued Dick, with a sidelong glance at Dorothy, who stood near by, appalled at his daring, "the best is none too good for common use. If my heart breaks the bonds of conventional restraint, and I call you by the name under which you always appear to me in my longing dreams, why should you not be gracious, and forgive me? Be kind to me, Sally, be just a little kind, and throw together a pan of those biscuits in your own inimitable style!"

"Run along with you, you limb of Satan," cried Mrs. Smithers, brandishing a floury spoon.

"Come along, Dorothy," said Dick, laying a huge but friendly paw upon Mrs. Carr's shoulder; "we're chased out." He put his head back into the kitchen, however, to file a parting petition for biscuits, which was unnecessary, for Mrs. Smithers had already found her rolling-pin and had begun to sift her flour.

Outside, he duly admired Maud, who was chewing the cud of reflection under a tree, created a panic in the chicken yard by lifting Abdul Hamid ignominiously by the legs, to see how heavy he was, and chased Claudius Tiberius under the barn.

"If that cat turns up missing some day," he said, "don't blame me. He looks so much like Uncle Ebeneezer that I can't stand for him."

"There's something queer about Claudius, anyway," ventured Dorothy. "Mrs. Smithers says that uncle killed him the week before he died, and——"

"Before who died?"

"Claudius—no, before uncle died, and she buried him, and he's come to life again."

"Uncle, or Claudius?"

"Claudius, you goose," laughed Dorothy.

"If I knew just how nearly related we were," remarked Dick, irrelevantly enough, "I believe I'd kiss you. You look so pretty with all your dimples hung out and your hair blowing in the wind."

Dorothy glanced up, startled, and inclined to be angry, but it was impossible to take offence at such a mischievous youth as Dick was at that moment. "We're not related," she said, coolly, "except by marriage."

"Well, that's near enough," returned Dick, who was never disposed to be unduly critical. "Your husband is only related to you by marriage. Don't be such a prude. Come to the waiting arms of your uncle, or cousin, or brother-in-law, or whatever it is that I happen to be."

"Go and kiss your friend Sally in the kitchen," laughed Dorothy. "You have my permission." Dick made a wry face. "I don't hanker to do it," he said, "but if you want me to, I will. I suppose she isn't pleased with her place and you want to make it more homelike for her."

"What relation were you to Uncle Ebeneezer?" queried Dorothy, curiously.

"Uncle and I," sighed Dick, "were connected by the closest ties of blood and marriage. Nobody could be more related than we were. I was the only child of Aunt Rebecca's sister's husband's sister's husband's sister. Say, on the dead, if I ever bother you will you tell me so and invite me to skip?"

"Of course I will."

"Shake hands on it, then; that's a good fellow. And say, did you say there was another skirt stopping here?"

"A—a what?"

"Petticoat," explained Dick, patiently; "mulier, as the ancient dagoes had it. They've been getting mulier ever since, too. How old is she?"

"Oh," answered Dorothy. "She's not more than twenty or twenty-one." Then, endeavouring to be just to Elaine, she added: "And a very pretty girl, too."

"Lead me to her," exclaimed Dick ecstatically. "Already she is mine!"

"You'll see her at luncheon. There's the bell, now."

Mr. Chester was duly presented to Miss St. Clair, and from then on, appeared to be on his good behaviour. Elaine's delicate, fragile beauty appealed strongly to the susceptible Dick, and from the very beginning, he was afraid of her—a dangerous symptom, if he had only known it.

Harlan, making the best of a bad bargain, devoted himself to his guests impartially, and, upon the whole, the luncheon went off very well, though the atmosphere was not wholly festive.

Afterward, when they sat down in the parlour, there was an awkward pause which no one seemed inclined to relieve. At length Dorothy, mindful of her duty as hostess, asked Miss St. Clair if she would not play something.

Willingly enough, Elaine went to the melodeon, which had not been opened since the Carrs came to live at the Jack-o'-Lantern, and lifted the lid. Immediately, however, she went off into hysterics, which were so violent that Harlan and Dorothy were obliged to assist her to her room.

Dick strongly desired to carry Elaine upstairs, but was forbidden by the hampering conventionalities. So he lounged over to the melodeon, somewhat surprised to find that "It" was still there.

"It" was a brown, wavy, false front of human hair, securely anchored to the keys underneath by a complicated system of loops of linen thread. Pinned to the top was a faded slip of paper on which Uncle Ebeneezer had written, long ago: "Mrs. Judson always kept her best false front in the melodeon. I do not desire to have it disturbed.—E. J."

"His Nibs never could bear music," thought Dick, as he closed the instrument, little guessing that a vein of sentiment in Uncle Ebeneezer's hard nature had impelled him to keep the prosaic melodeon forever sacred to the slender, girlish fingers that had last brought music from its yellowed keys.

From upstairs still came the sound of crying, which was not altogether to be wondered at, considering Miss St. Clair's weak, nervous condition. Harlan came down, scowling, and took back the brandy flask, moving none too hastily. "They don't like Elaine," murmured Dick to himself, vaguely troubled. "I wonder why—oh, I wonder why!"

# VIII

# More

Blue as sapphires were the eyes of Elaine, and her fair cheek was like that of an apple blossom. Set like a rose upon pearl was the dewy, fragrant sweetness of her mouth, and her breath was that of the rose itself. Her hands—but how shall I write of the flower-like hands of Elaine? They seemed all too frail to hold the reins of her palfrey, much less to guide him along the rocky road that lay before her.

Safely sheltered in a sunny valley was the Castle of Content, wherein Elaine's father reigned as Lord. Upon the hills close at hand were the orchards, which were now in bloom. A faint, unearthly sweetness came with every passing breeze, and was wafted through the open windows of the Castle, where, upon the upper floor, Elaine was wont to sit with her maids at the tapestry frames.

But, of late, a strange restlessness was upon her, and the wander-lust surged through her veins.

"My father," she said, "I am fain to leave the Castle of Content, and set out upon the Heart's Quest. Among the gallant knights of thy retinue, there is none whom I would wed, and it is seemly that I should set out to find my lord and master, for behold, father, as thou knowest, twenty years and more have passed over my head, and my beauty hath begun to fade."

The Lord of the Castle of Content smiled in amusement, that Elaine, the beautiful, should fancy her charms were on the wane. But he was ever eager to gratify the slightest wish of this only child of his, and so he gave his ready consent.

"Indeed, Elaine," he answered, "and if thou choosest, thou shalt go, but these despised knights shall attend thee, and also our new fool, who hath come from afar to make merry in our court. His motley is of an unfamiliar pattern, his quips and jests savour not so much of antiquity, and his songs are pleasing. He shall lighten the rigours of thy journey and cheer thee when thou art sad."

"But, father, I do not choose to have the fool."

"Say no more, Elaine, for if thou goest, thou shall have the fool. It is most fitting that in thy retinue there shouldst be more than one to wear the cap and bells, and it is in my mind to consider this quest of thine somewhat more than mildly foolish. Unnumbered brave and faithful knights are at thy feet and yet *thou canst not choose, but must needs fare onward in search of a stranger to be thy lord and master."*

*Elaine raised her hand. "As thou wilt, father," she said, submissively. "Thou canst not understand the way of a maid. Bid thy fool to prepare himself quickly for a long journey, since we start at sunset."*

*"But why at sunset, daughter? The way is long. Mayst not thy mission wait until sunrise?"*

*"Nay, father, for it is my desire to sleep to-night upon the ground. The tapestried walls of my chamber stifle me and I would fain lie in the fresh air with only the green leaves for my canopy and the stars for my taper lights."*

*"As thou wilt, Elaine, but my heart is sad at the prospect of losing thee. Thou art my only child, the image of thy dead mother, and my old eyes shall be misty for the sight of thee long before my gallant knights bring thee back again."*

*"So shall I gain some hours, father," she answered. "Perhaps my sunset journeying shall bring my return a day nearer. Cross me not in this wish, father, for it is my fancy to go."*

*So it was that the cavalcade was made ready and Elaine and her company left the Castle of Content at sunset. Two couriers rode at the head, to see that the way was clear, and with a silver bugle to warn travellers to stand aside until the Lady Elaine and her attendants had passed.*

*Upon a donkey, caparisoned in a most amusing manner, rode Le Jongleur, the new fool of whom the Lord of the Castle of Content had spoken. His motley, as has been said, was of an unfamiliar pattern, but was none the less striking, being made wholly of scarlet and gold. The Lady Elaine could not have guessed that it was assumed as a tribute to the trappings of her palfrey, for Le Jongleur's heart was most humble and loyal, though leaping now with the joy of serving the fair Lady Elaine.*

*The Lord of Content stood at the portal of the Castle to bid the retinue Godspeed, and as the cymbals crashed out a sounding farewell, he impatiently wiped away the mist, which already had clouded his vision. Long he waited, straining his eyes toward the distant cliffs, where, one by one, the company rode upward. The valley was in shadow, but the long light lay upon the hills, changing the crags to a wonder of purple and gold. To him, too, came the breath of apple bloom, but it brough no joy to his troubled heart.*

*What dangers lay in wait for Elaine as she fared forth upon her wild quest? What monsters haunted the primeval forests through which her path must lie? And where was the knight who should claim her innocent and maidenly heart? At this thought, the Lord of Content shuddered, then was quickly ashamed.*

57

*"I am as foolish," he muttered, "as he in motley, who rides at the side of Elaine. Surely my daughter, the child of a soldier, can make no unworthy choice."*

*The cavalcade had reached the summit of the cliff, now, and at the brink, turned back. The cymbals and the bugles pealed forth another sounding farewell to the Lord of the Castle of Content, whom Elaine well knew was waiting in the shadow of the portal till her company should be entirely lost to sight.*

*The last light shone upon the wonderful mass of gold which rippled to her waist, unbound, from beneath her close-fitting scarlet cap, and gave her an unearthly beauty. Le Jongleur held aloft his bauble, making it to nod in merry fashion, but the Lord of Content did not see, his eyes being fixed upon Elaine. She waved her hand to him, but he could not answer, for his shoulders were shaking with grief, nor, indeed, across the merciless distance that lay between, could he guess at Elaine's whispered prayer: "Dear Heavenly Father, keep thou my earthly father safe and happy, till his child comes back again."*

*Over the edge of the cliff and out upon a wide plain they fared. Ribbons of glorious colour streamed from the horizon to the zenith, and touched to flame the cymbals and the bugles and the trappings of the horses and the shields of the knights. Piercingly sweet, across the fields of blowing clover, came the even song of a feathered chorister, and*—what on earth was that noise?

Harlan went to the window impatiently, like one wakened from a dream by a blind impulse of action.

The village stage, piled high with trunks, was at his door, and from the cavernous depths of the vehicle, shrieks of juvenile terror echoed and re-echoed unceasingly. Mr. Blake, driving, merely waited in supreme unconcern.

"What in the hereafter," muttered Harlan, savagely. "More old lovers of Dorothy's, I suppose, or else the—Good Lord, it's twins!"

A child of four or five fell out of the stage, followed by another, who lit unerringly on top of the prostrate one. In the meteoric moment of the fall, Harlan had seen that the two must have discovered America at about the same time, for they were exactly alike, making due allowance for the slight difference made by masculine and feminine attire.

An enormous doll, which to Harlan's troubled sight first appeared to be an infant in arms, was violently ejected from the stage and added to the human pile which was wriggling and weeping upon the gravelled walk. A cub of seven next leaped out, whistling shrilly, then came a querulous, wailing, feminine voice from the interior.

"Willie," it whined, "how can you act so? Help your little brother and sister up and get Rebbie's doll."

To this the lad paid no attention whatever, and the mother herself assorted the weeping pyramid on the walk. Harlan ran downstairs, feeling that the hour had come to defend his hearthstone from outsiders. Dick and Dorothy were already at the door.

"Foundlings' Home," explained Dick, briefly, with a wink at Harlan. "They're late this year."

Dorothy was speechless with amazement and despair. Before Harlan had begun to think connectedly, one of the twins had darted into the house and bumped its head on the library door, thereupon making the Jack-o'-Lantern hideous with much lamentation.

The mother, apparently tired out, came in as though she had left something of great value there and had come to get it, pausing only to direct Harlan to pay the stage driver, and have her trunks taken into the rooms opening off the dining-room on the south side.

Willie took a mouth-organ out of his pocket and rendered a hitherto unknown air upon it with inimitable vigour. In the midst of the confusion, Claudius Tiberius had the misfortune to appear, and, immediately perceiving his mistake, whisked under the sofa, from whence the other twin determinedly haled him, using the handle which Nature had evidently intended for that purpose.

"Will you kindly tell me," demanded Mrs. Carr, when she could make herself heard, "what is the meaning of all this?"

"I do not understand you," said the mother of the twins, coldly. "Were you addressing me?"

"I was," returned Mrs. Carr, to Dick's manifest delight. "I desire to know why you have come to my house, uninvited, and made all this disturbance."

"The idea!" exclaimed the woman, trembling with anger. "Will you please send for Mr. Judson?"

"Mr. Judson," said Dorothy, icily, "has been dead for some time. This house is the property of my husband."

"Indeed! And who may your husband be?" The tone of the question did not indicate even faint interest in the subject under discussion.

Dorothy turned, but Harlan had long since beat an ignominious retreat, closely followed by Dick, whose idea, as audibly expressed, was that the women be allowed to "fight it out by themselves."

"I can readily understand," went on Dorothy, with a supreme effort at self-control, "that you have made a mistake for which you are not in any sense to blame. You are tired from your journey, and you are quite welcome to stay until to-morrow."

"To-morrow!" shrilled the woman. "I guess you don't know who I am! I am Mrs. Holmes, Rebecca Judson's own cousin, and I have spent the Summer here ever since Rebecca was married! I guess if Ebeneezer knew you were practically ordering his wife's own cousin out of his house, he'd rise from his grave to haunt you!"

Dorothy fancied that Uncle Ebeneezer's portrait moved slightly. Aunt Rebecca still surveyed the room from the easel, gentle, sweet-faced, and saintly. There was no resemblance whatever between Aunt Rebecca and the sallow, hollow-cheeked, wide-eyed termagant, with a markedly receding chin, who stood before Mrs. Carr and defied her.

"This is my husband's house," suggested Dorothy, pertinently.

"Then let your husband do the talking," rejoined Mrs. Holmes, sarcastically. "If he was sure it was his, I guess he wouldn't have run away. I've always had my own rooms here, and I intend to go and come as I please, as I always have done. You can't make me believe that Ebeneezer gave my apartments to your husband, nor him either, and I wouldn't advise any of you to try it."

Sounds of fearful panic came from the chicken yard, and Dorothy rushed out, swiftly laying avenging hands on the disturber of the peace. One of the twins was chasing Abdul Hamid around the coop with a lath, as he explained between sobs, "to make him lay." Mrs. Holmes bore down upon Dorothy before any permanent good had been done.

"How dare you!" she cried. "How dare you lay hands on my child! Come, Ebbie, come to mamma. Bless his little heart, he shall chase the chickens if he wants to, so there, there. Don't cry, Ebbie. Mamma will get you another lath and you shall play with the chickens all the afternoon. There, there!"

Harlan appeared at this juncture, and in a few quiet, well-chosen words told Mrs. Holmes that the chicken coop was his property, and that neither now nor at any other time should any one enter it without his express permission.

"Upon my word," remarked Mrs. Holmes, still soothing the unhappy twin. "How high and mighty we are when we're living off our poor dead uncle's bounty! Telling his wife's own cousin what she's to do, and what she isn't! Upon my word!"

So saying, Mrs. Holmes retired to the house, her pace hastened by howls from the other twin, who was in trouble with her older brother somewhere in her "apartment."

Dorothy looked at Harlan, undecided whether to laugh or to cry. "Poor little woman," he said, softly; "don't you fret. We'll have them out of the house no later than to-morrow."

"All of them?" asked Dorothy, eagerly, as Miss St. Clair strolled into the front yard.

Harlan's brow clouded and he shifted uneasily from one foot to the other. "I don't know," he said, slowly, "whether I've got nerve enough to order a woman out of my house or not. Let's wait and see what happens."

A sob choked Dorothy, and she ran swiftly into the house, fortunately meeting no one on her way to her room. Dick ventured out of the barn and came up to Harlan, who was plainly perplexed.

"Very, very mild arrival," commented Mr. Chester, desiring to put his host at his ease. "I've never known 'em to come so peacefully as they have to-day. Usually there's more or less disturbance."

"Disturbance," repeated Harlan. "Haven't we had a disturbance to-day?"

"We have not," answered Dick, placidly. "Wait till young Ebeneezer and Rebecca get more accustomed to their surroundings, and then you'll have a Fourth of July every day, with Christmas, Thanksgiving, and St. Patrick's Day thrown in. Willie is the worst little terror that ever went unlicked, and the twins come next."

"Perhaps you don't understand children," remarked Harlan, with a patronising air, and more from a desire to disagree with Dick than from anything else. "I've always liked them."

"If you have," commented Dick, with a knowing chuckle, "you're in a fair way to get cured of it."

"Tell me about these people," said Harlan, ignoring the speech, and dominated once more by healthy human curiosity. "Who are they and where do they come from?"

"They're dwellers from the infernal regions," explained Dick, with an air of truthfulness, "and they came from there because the old Nick turned 'em out. They were upsetting things and giving the place a bad name. Mrs. Holmes says she's Aunt Rebecca's cousin, but nobody knows whether she is or not. She's come here every Summer since Aunt Rebecca died, and poor old uncle couldn't help himself. He hinted more than once that he'd enjoy her absence if she could be moved to make herself scarce, but it had no more effect than a snowflake would in the place she came from. The most he could do was to build a wing on the house with a separate kitchen and dining-room in it, and take his own meals in the library, with the door bolted.

"Willie is a Winter product and Judson Centre isn't a pleasant place in the cold months, but the twins were born here, five years ago this Summer. They came in the night, but didn't make any more trouble then than they have every day since."

"What would you do?" asked Harlan, after a thoughtful silence, "if you were in my place?"

"I'd be tickled to death because a kind Providence had married me to Dorothy instead of to Mrs. Holmes. Poor old Holmes is in his well-earned grave."

With great dignity, Harlan walked into the house, but Dick, occupied with his own thoughts, did not guess that his host was offended.

After the first excitement was over, comparative peace settled down upon the Jack-o'-Lantern. Mrs. Holmes decided the question of where she should eat, by setting four more places at the table when Mrs. Smithers's back was turned. Dorothy did not appear at luncheon, and Mrs. Smithers performed her duties with such pronounced ungraciousness that Elaine felt as though something was about to explode.

A long sleep, born of nervous exhaustion, came at last to Dorothy's relief. When she awoke, it was night and the darkness dazed her at first. She sat up and rubbed her eyes, wondering whether she had been dead, or merely ill.

There was not a sound in the Jack-o'-Lantern, and the events of the day seemed like some hideous nightmare which waking had put to rout. She bathed her face in cool water, then went to look out of the window.

A lantern moved back and forth under the trees in the orchard, and a tall, dark figure, armed with a spade, accompanied it. "It's Harlan," thought Dorothy. "I'll go down and see what he's burying."

But it was only Mrs. Smithers, who appeared much startled when she saw her mistress at her side.

"What are you doing?" demanded Dorothy, seeing that Mrs. Smithers had dug a hole at least a foot and a half each way.

"Just a-satisfyin' myself," explained the handmaiden, with a note of triumph in her voice, "about that there cat. 'Ere's where I buried 'im, and 'ere's where there ain't no signs of 'is dead body. 'E's come back to 'aunt us, that's wot 'e 'as, and your uncle'll be the next."

"Don't be so foolish," snapped Dorothy. "You've forgotten the place, that's all, and I don't wish to hear any more of this nonsense."

"'Oo was it?" asked Mrs. Smithers, "as come out of a warm bed at midnight to see as if folks wot was diggin' for cats found anythink? 'T warn't me, Miss, that's wot it warn't, and I take it that them as follers is as nonsensical as them wot digs. Anyhow, Miss, 'ere's where 'e was buried, and 'ere's where 'e ain't now. You can think wot you likes, that's wot you can."

Claudius Tiberius suddenly materialised out of the surrounding darkness, and after sniffing at the edge of the hole, jumped in to investigate.

"You see that, Miss?" quavered Mrs. Smithers. "'E knows where 'e's been, and 'e knows where 'e ain't now."

"Mrs. Smithers," said Dorothy, sternly, "will you kindly fill up that hole and come into the house and go to bed? I don't want to be kept awake all night."

"You don't need to be kept awake, Miss," said Mrs. Smithers, slowly filling up the hole. "The worst is 'ere already and wot's comin' is comin' anyway, and besides," she added, as an afterthought, "there ain't a blessed one of 'em come 'ere at night since your uncle fixed over the house."

# IX

# Another

For the first time in her life, Mrs. Carr fully comprehended the sensations of a wild animal caught in a trap. In her present painful predicament, she was absolutely helpless, and she realised it. It was Harlan's house, as he had said, but so powerful and penetrating was the personality of the dead man that she felt as though it was still largely the property of Uncle Ebeneezer.

The portrait in the parlour gave her no light upon the subject, though she studied it earnestly. The face was that of an old man, soured and embittered by what Life had brought him, who seemed now to have a peculiarly malignant aspect. Dorothy fancied, in certain morbid moments, that Uncle Ebeneezer, from some safe place, was keenly relishing the whole situation.

Upon her soul, too, lay heavily that ancient Law of the House, which demands unfailing courtesy to the stranger within our gates. Just why the eating of our bread and salt by some undesired guest should exert any particular charm of immunity, has long been an open question, but the Law remains.

She felt, dimly, that the end was not yet—that still other strangers were coming to the Jack-o'-Lantern for indefinite periods. She saw, now, why wing after wing had been added to the house, but could not understand the odd arrangement of the front windows. Through some inner sense of loyalty to Uncle Ebeneezer, she forebore to question either Mrs. Smithers or Dick—two people who could probably have given her some light on the subject. She had gathered, however, from hints dropped here and there, as well as from the overpowering evidence of recent events, that a horde of relatives swarmed each Summer at the queer house on the hilltop and remained until late Autumn.

Harlan said nothing, and nowadays Dorothy saw very little of him. Most of the time he was at work in the library, or else taking long, solitary rambles through the surrounding country. At meals he was moody and taciturn, his book obliterating all else from his mind.

He doubtless knew, subconsciously, that his house was disturbed by alien elements, but he dwelt too securely in the upper regions to be troubled by the obvious fact. Once in the library, with every door securely bolted, he could afford to laugh at the tumult outside, if, indeed, he should ever become aware of its existence. The children might make the very air vocal with their howls,

Elaine might have hysterics, Mrs. Smithers render hymns in a cracked, squeaky voice, and Dick whistle eternally, but Harlan was in a strange new country, with a beautiful lady, a company of gallant knights, and a jester.

The rest was all unreal. He seemed to see people through a veil, to hear what they said without fully comprehending it, and to walk through his daily life blindly, without any sort of emotion. Worst of all, Dorothy herself seemed detached and dream-like. He saw that her face was white and her eyes sad, but it affected him not at all. He had yet to learn that in this, as in everything else, a price must inevitably be paid, and that the sudden change of all his loved realities to hazy visions was the terrible penalty of his craft.

Yet there was compensation, which is also inevitable. To him, the book was vital, reaching down into the very heart of the world. Fancy took his work, and, to the eyes of its creator, made it passing fair. At times he would sit for an hour or more, nibbling at the end of his pencil, only negatively conscious, like one who stares fixedly at a blank wall. Presently, Elaine and her company would come back again, and he would go on with them, writing down only what he saw and felt.

Chapter after chapter was written and tossed feverishly aside. The words beat in his pulses like music, each one with its own particular significance. In return for his personal effacement came moments of supremest joy, when his whole world was aflame with light, and colour, and sound, and his physical body fairly shook with ecstasy.

Little did he know that the Cup was in his hands, and that he was draining it to the very dregs of bitterness. For this temporary intoxication, he must pay in every hour of his life to come. Henceforward he was set apart from his fellows, painfully isolated, eternally alone. He should have friends, but only for the hour. The stranger in the street should be the same to him as one he had known for many years, and he should be equally ready, at any moment, to cast either aside. With a quick, merciless insight, like the knife of a surgeon used without an anæsthetic, he should explore the inmost recesses of every personality with which he came in contact, involuntarily, and find himself interested only as some new trait or capacity was revealed. Calm and emotionless, urged by some hidden power, he should try each individual to see of what he was made; observing the man under all possible circumstances, and at times enmeshing new circumstances about him. He should sacrifice himself continually if by so doing he could find the deep roots of the other man's selfishness, and, conversely, be utterly selfish if necessary to discover the other's power of self-sacrifice.

Unknowingly, he had ceased to be a man and had become a ferret. It was no light payment exacted in return for the pleasure of writing about Elaine. He had the ability to live in any place or century he pleased, but he had paid for it by putting his present reality upon precisely the same footing. Detachment was his continually. Henceforth he was a spectator merely, without any particular concern in what passed before his eyes. Some people he should know at a glance, others in a week, a month, or a year. Across the emptiness between them, some one should clasp his hand, yet share no more his inner life than one who lies beside a dreamer and thinks thus to know where the other wanders on the strange trails of sleep.

In the dregs of the Cup lay the potential power to cast off his present life as a mollusk leaves his shell, and as completely forget it. For Love, and Death, and Pain are only symbols to him who is enslaved by the pen. Moreover, he suffers always the pangs of an unsatisfied hunger, the exquisite torture of an unappeased and unappeasable thirst, for something which, like a will-o'-the-wisp, hovers ever above and beyond him, past the power of words to interpret or express.

It is often reproachfully said that one "makes copy" of himself and his friends—that nothing is too intimately sacred to be seized upon and dissected in print. Not so long ago, it was said that a certain man was "botanising on his mother's grave," a pardonable confusion, perhaps, of facts and realities. The bitter truth is that the writer lives his books—and not much else. From title to colophon, he escapes no pang, misses no joy. The life of the book is his from beginning to end. At the close of it, he has lived what his dream people have lived and borne the sorrows of half a dozen entire lifetimes, mercilessly concentrated into the few short months of writing.

One by one, his former pleasures vanish. Even the divine consolation of books is partly if not wholly gone. Behind the printed page, he sees ever the machinery of composition, the preparation for climax, the repetition in its proper place, the introduction and interweaving of major and minor, of theme and contrast. For the fine, glowing fancy of the other man has not appeared in his book, and to the eye of the fellow-craftsman only the mechanism is there. Mask-like, the author stands behind his Punch-and-Judy box, twitching the strings that move his marionettes, heedless of the fact that in his audience there must be a few who know him surely for what he is.

If only the transfiguring might of the Vision could be put into print, there would be little in the world save books. Happily heedless of the mockery of it all, Harlan laboured on, destined fully to sense his entire payment much later, suffer vicariously for a few hours on account of it, then to forget.

Dorothy, meanwhile, was learning a hard lesson. Harlan's changeless preoccupation hurt her cruelly, but, woman-like, she considered it a manifestation of genius and endeavoured to be proud accordingly. It had not occurred to her that there could ever be anything in Harlan's thought into which she was not privileged to go. She had thought of marriage as a sort of miraculous welding of two individualities into one, and was perceiving that it changed nothing very much; that souls went on their way unaltered. She saw, too, that there was no one in the wide world who could share her every mood and tense, that ultimately each one of us lives and dies alone, within the sanctuary of his own inner self, cheered only by some passing mood of friend or stranger, which chances to chime with his.

It was Dick who, blindly enough, helped her over many a hard place, and quickened her sense of humour into something upon which she might securely lean. He was too young and too much occupied with the obvious to look further, but he felt that Dorothy was troubled, and that it was his duty, as a man and a gentleman, to cheer her up.

Privately, he considered Harlan an amiable kind of a fool, who shut himself up needlessly in a musty library when he might be outdoors, or talking with a charming woman, or both. When he discovered that Harlan had hitherto earned his living by writing and hoped to continue doing it, he looked upon his host with profound pity. Books, to Dick, were among the things which kept life from being wholly pleasant and agreeable. He had gone through college because otherwise he would have been separated from his friends, and because a small legacy from a distant relative, who had considerately died at an opportune moment, enabled him to pay for his tuition and his despised books.

"I was never a pig, though," he explained to Dorothy, in a confidential moment. "There was one chump in our class who wanted to know all there was in the book, and made himself sick trying to cram it in. All of a sudden, he graduated. He left college feet first, three on a side, with the class walking slow behind him. I never was like that. I was sort of an epicure when it came to knowledge, tasting delicately here and there, and never greedy. Why, as far back as when I was studying algebra, I nobly refused to learn the binomial theorem. I just read it through once, hastily, like taking one sniff at a violet, and then let it alone. The other fellows fairly gorged themselves with it, but I didn't—I had too much sense."

When Mr. Chester had been there a week, he gave Dorothy two worn and crumpled two-dollar bills.

"What's this?" she asked, curiously. "Where did you find it?"

"'Find it' is good," laughed Dick. "I earned it, my dear lady, in hard and uncongenial toil. It's my week's board."

"You're not going to pay any board here. You're a guest."

"Not on your life. You don't suppose I'm going to sponge my keep off anybody, do you? I paid Uncle Ebeneezer board right straight along and there's no reason why I shouldn't pay you. You can put that away in your sock, or wherever it is that women keep money, or else I take the next train. If you don't want to lose me, you have to accept four plunks every Monday. I've got lots of four plunks," he added, with a winning smile.

"Very well," said Dorothy, quite certain that she could not spare Dick. "If it will make you feel any better about staying, I'll take it."

He had quickly made friends with Elaine, and the three made a more harmonious group than might have been expected under the circumstances. With returning strength and health, Miss St. Clair began to take more of an interest in her surroundings. She gathered the white clover blossoms in which Dorothy tied up her pats of sweet butter, picked berries in the garden, skimmed the milk, helped churn, and fed the chickens.

Dick took entire charge of the cow, thus relieving Mrs. Smithers of an uncongenial task and winning her heartfelt gratitude. She repaid him with unnumbered biscuits of his favourite kind and with many a savoury "snack" between meals. He also helped Dorothy in many other ways. It was Dick who collected the eggs every morning and took them to the sanitarium, along with such other produce as might be ready for the market. He secured astonishing prices for the things he sold, and set it down to man's superior business ability when questioned by his hostess. Dorothy never guessed that most of the money came out of his own pocket, and was charged up, in the ragged memorandum book which he carried, to "Elaine's board."

Miss St. Clair had never thought of offering compensation, and no one suggested it to her, but Dick privately determined to make good the deficiency, sure that a woman married to "a writing chump" would soon be in need of ready money if not actually starving at the time. That people should pay for what Harlan wrote seemed well-nigh incredible. Besides, though Dick had never read that "love is an insane desire on the part of a man to pay a woman's board bill for life," he took a definite satisfaction out of this secret expenditure, which he did not stop to analyse.

He brought back full price for everything he took to the "repair-shop," as he had irreverently christened the sanitarium, though he seldom sold much. On the other side of the hill he had a small but select graveyard where he buried such unsalable articles as he could not eat. His appetite was capricious, and Dorothy had frequently observed that when he came back from the long walk to the sanitarium, he ate nothing at all.

He established a furniture factory under a spreading apple tree at a respectable distance from the house, and began to remodel the black-walnut relics which were evidence of his kinsman's poor taste. He took many a bed apart, scraped off the disfiguring varnish, sandpapered and oiled the wood, and put it together in new and beautiful forms. He made several tables, a cabinet, a bench, half a dozen chairs, a set of hanging shelves, and even aspired to a desk, which, owing to the limitations of the material, was not wholly successful.

Dorothy and Elaine sat in rocking-chairs under the tree and encouraged him while he worked. One of them embroidered a simple design upon a burlap curtain while the other read aloud, and together they planned a shapely remodelling of the Jack-o'-Lantern. Fortunately, the woodwork was plain, and the ceilings not too high.

"I think," said Elaine, "that the big living room with the casement windows will be perfectly beautiful. You couldn't have anything lovelier than this dull walnut with the yellow walls."

Whatever Mrs. Carr's thoughts might be, this simple sentence was usually sufficient to turn the current into more pleasant channels. She had planned to have needless partitions taken out, and make the whole lower floor into one room, with only a dining-room, kitchen, and pantry back of it. She would take up the unsightly carpets, over which impossible plants wandered persistently, and have them woven into rag rugs, with green and brown and yellow borders. The floor was to be stained brown and the pine woodwork a soft, old green. Yellow walls and white net curtains, with the beautiful furniture Dick was making, completed a very charming picture in the eyes of a woman who loved her home.

Outspeeding it in her fancy was the finer, truer living which she believed lay beyond. Some day she and Harlan, alone once more, with the cobwebs of estrangement swept away, should begin a new and happier honeymoon in the transformed house. When the book was done—ah, when the book was done! But he was not reading any part of it to her now and would not let her begin copying it on the typewriter.

"I'll do it myself, when I'm ready," he said, coldly. "I can use a typewriter just as well as you can."

Dorothy sighed, unconsciously, for the woman's part is always to wait patiently while men achieve, and she who has learned to wait patiently, and be happy meanwhile, has learned the finest art of all—the art of life.

"Now," said Dick, "that's a peach of a table, if I do say it as shouldn't."

They readily agreed with him, for it was low and massive, built on simple, dignified lines, and beautifully finished. The headboards of three ponderous walnut beds and the supporting columns of a hideous sideboard had gone into its composition, thus illustrating, as Dorothy said, that ugliness may be changed to beauty by one who knows how and is willing to work for it.

The noon train whistled shrilly in the distance, and Dorothy started out of her chair. "She's afraid," laughed Dick, instantly comprehending. "She's afraid somebody is coming on it."

"More twins?" queried Elaine, from the depths of her rocker. "Surely there can't be any more twins?"

"I don't know," answered Dorothy, vaguely troubled. "Someway, I feel as though something terrible were going to happen."

Nothing happened, however, until after luncheon, just as she had begun to breathe peacefully again. Willie saw the procession first and ran back with gleeful shouts to make the announcement. So it was that the entire household, including Harlan, formed a reception committee on the front porch.

Up the hill, drawn by two straining horses, came what appeared at first to be a pyramid of furniture, but later resolved itself into the component parts of a more ponderous bed than the ingenuity of man had yet contrived. It was made of black walnut, and was at least three times as heavy as any of those in the Jack-o'-Lantern. On the top of the mass was perched a little old man in a skull cap, a slippered foot in a scarlet sock airily waving at one side. A bright green coil closely clutched in his withered hands was the bed cord appertaining to the bed—a sainted possession from which its owner sternly refused to part.

"By Jove!" shouted Dick; "it's Uncle Israel and his crib!"

Paying no heed to the assembled group, Uncle Israel dismounted nimbly enough, and directed the men to take his bed upstairs, which they did, while Harlan and Dorothy stood by helplessly. Here, under his profane and involved direction, the structure was finally set in place, even to the patchwork quilt, fearfully and wonderfully made, which surmounted it all.

Financial settlement was waved aside by Uncle Israel as a matter in which he was not interested, and it was Dick who counted out two dimes and a nickel to secure peace. A supplementary procession appeared with a small, weather-beaten trunk, a folding bath-cabinet, and a huge case which, from Uncle Israel's perturbation, evidently contained numerous fragile articles of great value.

"Tell Ebeneezer," wheezed the newcomer, "that I have arrived."

"Ebeneezer," replied Dick, in wicked imitation of the old man's asthmatic speech, "has been dead for some time."

"Then," creaked Uncle Israel, waving a tremulous, bony hand suggestively toward the door, "kindly leave me alone with my grief."

# X

## Still More

Uncle Israel, whose other name was Skiles, adjusted himself to his grief in short order. The sounds which issued from his room were not those commonly associated with mourning. Dick, fully accustomed to various noises, explained them for the edification of the Carrs, who at present were sorely in need of edification.

"That's the bath cabinet," remarked Mr. Chester, with the air of a connoisseur. "He's setting it up near enough to the door so that if anybody should come in unexpectedly while it's working, the whole thing will be tipped over and the house set on fire. Uncle Israel won't have any lock or bolt on his door for fear he should die in the night. He relies wholly on the bath cabinet and moral suasion. Nobody knocks on doors here, anyway—just goes in.

"That's his trunk. He keeps it under the window. The bed is set up first, then the bath cabinet, then the trunk, and last, but not least, the medicine chest. He keeps his entire pharmacopœia on a table at the head of his bed, with a candle and matches, so that if he feels badly in the night, the proper remedy is instantly at hand. He prepares some of his medicines himself, but he isn't bigoted about it. He buys the rest at wholesale, and I'll eat my hat if he hasn't got a full-sized bottle of every patent medicine that's on sale anywhere in the United States."

"How old," asked Harlan, speaking for the first time, "is Uncle Israel?"

"Something over ninety, I believe," returned Dick. "I've lost my book of vital statistics, so I don't know, exactly."

"How long," inquired Dorothy, with a forced smile, "does Uncle Israel stay?"

"Lord bless you, my dear lady, Uncle Israel stays all Summer. Hello—there are some more!"

A private conveyance of uncertain age and purposes drew up before the door. From it dismounted a very slender young man of medium height, whose long auburn hair hung over his coat-collar and at times partially obscured his soulful grey eyes. It resembled the mane of a lion, except in colour. He carried a small black valise, and a roll of manuscript tied with a badly soiled ribbon.

An old lady followed, stepping cautiously, but still finding opportunity to scrutinise the group in the doorway, peering sharply over her gold-bowed spectacles. It was she who paid the driver, and even before the two reached the house, it was evident that they were not on speaking terms.

The young man offered Mr. Chester a thin, tremulous hand which lay on Dick's broad palm in a nerveless, clammy fashion. "Pray," he said, in a high, squeaky voice, "convey my greetings to dear Uncle Ebeneezer, and inform him that I have arrived."

"I am at present holding no communication with Uncle Ebeneezer," explained Dick. "The wires are down."

"Where is Ebeneezer?" demanded the old lady.

"Dead," answered Dorothy, wearily; "dead, dead. He's been dead a long time. This is our house—he left it to my husband and me."

"Don't let that disturb you a mite," said the old lady, cheerfully. "I like your looks a whole lot, an' I'd just as soon stay with you as with Ebeneezer. I dunno but I'd ruther."

She must have been well past sixty, but her scanty hair was as yet untouched with grey. She wore it parted in the middle, after an ancient fashion, and twisted at the back into a tight little knob, from which the ends of a wire hairpin protruded threateningly. Dorothy reflected, unhappily, that the whole thing was done up almost tight enough to play a tune on.

For the rest, her attire was neat, though careless. One had always the delusion that part or all of it was on the point of coming off.

The young man was wiping his weak eyes upon a voluminous silk handkerchief which had evidently seen long service since its last washing. "Dear Uncle Ebeneezer," he breathed, running his long, bony fingers through his hair. "I cannot tell you how heavily this blow falls upon me. Dear Uncle Ebeneezer was a distinguished patron of the arts. Our country needs more men like him, men with fine appreciation, vowed to the service of the Ideal. If you will pardon me, I will now retire to my apartment and remain there a short time in seclusion."

So saying, he ran lightly upstairs, as one who was thoroughly at home.

"Who in—" began Harlan.

"Mr. Harold Vernon Perkins, poet," said Dick. "He's got his rhyming dictionary and all his odes with him."

"Without knowing," said Dorothy, "I should have thought his name was Harold or Arthur or Paul. He looks it."

"It wa'n't my fault," interjected the old lady, "that he come. I didn't even sense that he was on the same train as me till I hired the carriage at the junction an' he clim' in. He said he might as well come along as we was both goin' to the same place, an' it would save him walkin', an' not cost me no more than 't would anyway."

While she was speaking, she had taken off her outer layer of drapery and her bonnet. "I'll just put these things in my room, my dear," she said to Dorothy, "an' then I'll come back an' talk to you. I like your looks first-rate."

"Who in—," said Harlan, again, as the old lady vanished into one of the lower wings.

"Mrs. Belinda something," answered Dick. "I don't know who she's married to now. She's had bad luck with her husbands."

Mrs. Carr, deeply troubled, was leaning against the wall in the hall, and Dick patted her hand soothingly. "Don't you fret," he said, cheerily; "I'm here to see you through."

"That being the case," remarked Harlan, with a certain acidity in his tone, "I'll go back to my work."

The old lady appeared again as Harlan slammed the library door, and suggested that Dick should go away.

"Polite hint," commented Mr. Chester, not at all disturbed. "See you later." He went out, whistling, with his cap on the back of his head and his hands in his pockets.

"I reckon you're a new relative, be n't you?" asked the lady guest, eyeing Dorothy closely. "I disremember seein' you before."

"I am Mrs. Carr," repeated Dorothy, mechanically. "My husband, Harlan Carr, is Uncle Ebeneezer's nephew, and the house was left to him."

"Do tell!" ejaculated the other. "I wouldn't have thought it of Ebeneezer. I'm Belinda Dodd, relict of Benjamin Dodd, deceased. How many are there here, my dear?"

"Miss St. Clair, Mr. Chester, Mrs. Holmes and her three children, Uncle Israel Skiles, and you two, besides Mr. Carr, Mrs. Smithers, and myself."

"Is that all?" asked the visitor, in evident surprise.

"All!" repeated Dorothy. "Isn't that enough?"

"Lord love you, my dear, it's plain to be seen that you ain't never been here before. Only them few an' so late in the season, too. Why, there's Cousin Si Martin, an' his wife, an' their eight children, some of the children bein' married an' havin' other children, an' Sister-in-law Fanny Wood with her invalid husband, her second husband, that is, an' Rebecca's Uncle James's third wife with her two daughters, an' Rebecca's sister's second husband with his new wife an' their little boy, an' Uncle Jason an' his stepson, the one that has fits, an' Cousin Sally Simmons an' her daughter, an' the four little Riley children an' their Aunt Lucretia, an' Step-cousin Betsey Skiles with her two nieces, though I misdoubt their comin' this year. The youngest niece had typhoid fever here last Summer for eight weeks, an' Betsey thinks the location ain't healthy, in spite of it's bein' so near the sanitarium. She was threatenin' to get the health department or somethin' after Ebeneezer an' have the drinkin' water looked into, so's they didn't part on the pleasantest terms, but in the main we've all got along well together.

"If Betsey knowed Ebeneezer was dead, she wouldn't hesitate none about comin', typhoid or no typhoid. Mebbe it was her fault some, for Ebeneezer wa'n't to blame for his drinkin' water no more 'n I'd be. Our minister used to say that there was no discipline for the soul like livin' with folks, year in an' year out hand-runnin', an' Betsey is naturally that kind. Ebeneezer always lived plain, but we're all simple folks, not carin' much for style, so we never minded it. The air's good up here an' I dunno any better place to spend the Summer. My gracious! You be n't sick, be you?"

"I don't know what to do," murmured Dorothy, her white lips scarcely moving; "I don't know what to do."

"Well, now," responded Mrs. Dodd, "I can see that I've upset you some. Perhaps you're one of them people that don't like to have other folks around you. I've heard of such, comin' from the city. Why, I knew a woman that lived in the city, an' she said she didn't know the name of the woman next door to her after livin' there over eight months,—an' their windows lookin' right into each other, too."

"I hate people!" cried Dorothy, in a passion of anger. "I don't want anybody here but my husband and Mrs. Smithers!"

"Set quiet, my dear, an' make your mind easy. I'm sure Ebeneezer never intended his death to make any difference in my spendin' the Summer here, especially when I'm fresh from another bereavement, but if you're in earnest about closin' your doors on your poor dead aunt's relations, why I'll see what I can do."

"Oh, if you could!" Dorothy almost screamed the words. "If you can keep any more people from coming here, I'll bless you for ever."

"Poor child, I can see that you're considerable upset. Just get me the pen an' ink an' some paper an' envelopes an' I'll set down right now an' write to the connection an' tell 'em that Ebeneezer's dead an' bein' of unsound mind at the last has willed the house to strangers who refuse to open their doors to the blood relations of poor dead Rebecca. That's all I can do an' I can't promise that it'll work. Ebeneezer writ several times to us all that he didn't feel like havin' no more company, but Rebecca's relatives was all of a forgivin' disposition an' never laid it up against him. We all kep' on a-comin' just the same."

"Tell them," cried Dorothy her eyes unusually bright and her cheeks burning, "that we've got smallpox here, or diphtheria, or a lunatic asylum, or anything you like. Tell them there's a big dog in the yard that won't let anybody open the gate. Tell them anything!"

"Just you leave it all to me, my dear," said Mrs. Dodd, soothingly. "On account of the connection bein' so differently constituted, I'll have to tell 'em all different. Disease would keep away some an' fetch others. Betsey Skiles, now, she feels to turn her hand to nursin' an' I've knowed her to go miles in the dead of Winter to set up with a stranger that had some disease she wa'n't familiar with. Dogs would bring others an' only scare a few. Just you leave it all to me. There ain't never no use in borrerin' trouble an' givin' up your peace of mind as security, 'cause you don't never get the security back. I've been married enough to know that there's plenty of trouble in life besides what's looked for, an' it'll get in, without your holdin' open the door an' spreadin' a mat out with 'Welcome' on it. Did Ebeneezer leave any property?"

"Only the house and furniture," answered Dorothy, feeling that the whole burden of the world had been suddenly shifted to her young shoulders.

"Rebecca had a big diamond pin," said Mrs. Dodd, after a brief silence, "that she allers said was to be mine when she got through with it. Ebeneezer give it to her for a weddin' present. You ain't seen it layin' around, have you?"

"No, I haven't seen it 'laying around,'" retorted Dorothy, conscious that she was juggling with the truth.

"Well," continued Mrs. Dodd, easily, nibbling her pen holder, "when it comes to light, just remember that it's mine. I don't doubt it'll turn up sometime. An' now, my dear, I'll just begin on them letters. Cousin Si Martin's folks are a-packin' an' expectin' to get here next week. I suppose you're willin' to furnish the stamps?"

"Willing!" cried Dorothy, "I should say yes!"

Mrs. Dodd toiled long at her self-imposed task, and, having finished it, went out into the kitchen, where for an hour or more she exchanged mortuary gossip with Mrs. Smithers, every detail of the conversation being keenly relished by both ladies.

At dinner-time, eleven people sat down to partake of the excellent repast furnished by Mrs. Smithers under the stimulus of pleasant talk. Harlan was at the head, with Miss St. Clair on his right and Mrs. Dodd on his left. Next to Miss St. Clair was the poet, whose deep sorrow did not interfere with his appetite. The twins were next to him, then Mrs. Holmes, then Willie, then

Dorothy, at the foot of the table. On her right was Dick, the space between Dick and Mrs. Dodd being occupied by Uncle Israel.

To a careless observer, it might have seemed that Uncle Israel had more than his share of the table, but such in reality was not the case. His plate was flanked by a goodly array of medicine bottles, and cups and bowls of predigested and patent food. Uncle Israel, as Dick concisely expressed it, was "pie for the cranks."

"My third husband," remarked Mrs. Dodd, pleasantly, well aware that she was touching her neighbour's sorest spot, "was terribly afflicted with stomach trouble."

"The only stomach trouble I've ever had," commented Mr. Chester, airily spearing another biscuit with his fork, "was in getting enough to put into it."

"Have a care, young man," wheezed Uncle Israel, warningly. "There ain't nothin' so bad for the system as hot bread."

"It would be bad for my system," resumed Dick, "not to be able to get it."

"My third husband," continued Mrs. Dodd, disregarding the interruption, "wouldn't have no bread in the house at all. He et these little straw mattresses, same as you've got, so constant that he finally died from the tic doleroo. Will you please pass me them biscuits, Mis' Carr?"

Mrs. Dodd was obliged to rise and reach past Uncle Israel, who declined to be contaminated by passing the plate, before she attained her desired biscuit.

"Next time, Aunt Belinda," said Dick, "I'll throw you one. Suffering Moses, what new dope is that?"

A powerful and peculiarly penetrating odour filled the room. Presently it became evident that Uncle Israel had uncorked a fresh bottle of medicine. Miss St. Clair coughed and hastily excused herself.

"It's time for me to take my pain-killer," murmured Uncle Israel, pouring out a tablespoonful of a thick, brown mixture. "This here cured a Congressman in less 'n half a bottle of a gnawin' pain in his vitals. I ain't never took none of it yet, but I aim to now."

The vapour of it had already made the twins cry and brought tears to Mrs. Dodd's eyes, but Uncle Israel took it clear and smacked his lips over it enjoyably. "It seems to be a searchin' medicine," he commented, after an interval of silence. "I don't misdoubt that it'll locate that pain that was movin' up and down my back all night last night."

Uncle Israel's wizened old face, with its fringe of white whisker, beamed with the joy of a scientist who has made a new and important discovery. He had a long, hooked nose, and was painfully near-sighted, but refused to wear glasses.

Just now he sniffed inquiringly at the open bottle of medicine. "Yes," he said, nodding his bald head sagely, "I don't misdoubt this here can locate it."

"I don't, either," said Harlan, grimly, putting his handkerchief to his nose. "Will you excuse me, Dorothy?"

"Certainly."

Mrs. Holmes took the weeping twins away from the table, and Willie, his mentor gone, began to eat happily with his fingers. The poet rose and drew a roll of manuscript from his coat pocket.

"This afternoon," he said, clearing his throat, "I employed my spare moments in composing an ode to the memory of our sainted relative, under whose hospitable roof we are all now so pleasantly gathered. I will read it to you."

Mrs. Dodd hastily left the table, muttering indistinctly, and Dick followed her. Willie slipped from his chair, crawled under the table, and by stealthily sticking a pin into Uncle Israel's ankle, produced a violent disturbance, during which the pain-killer was badly spilled. When the air finally cleared, there was no one in the room but the poet, who sadly rolled up his manuscript.

"I will read it at breakfast," he thought. "I will give them all the pleasure of hearing it. Art is for the many, not for the few. I must use it to elevate humanity to the Ideal."

He went back to his own room to add some final reverent touches to the masterpiece, and to meditate upon the delicate blonde beauty of Miss St. Clair.

From Mrs. Dodd, meanwhile, Dick had gathered the pleasing purport of her voluminous correspondence, and insisted on posting all the letters that very night, though morning would have done just as well. When he had gone downhill on his errand of mercy, whistling cheerily as was his wont, Mrs. Dodd went into her own room and locked the door, immediately beginning a careful search of the entire apartment.

She scrutinised the walls closely, and rapped softly here and there, listening intently for a hollow sound. Standing on a chair, she felt all along the mouldings and window-casings, taking unto herself much dust in the process. She spent half an hour in the stuffy closet, investigating the shelves and recesses, then she got down on her rheumatic old knees and crept laboriously over the carpet, systematically taking it breadth by breadth, and paying special attention to that section of it which was under the bed.

"When you've found where anythin' ain't," she said to herself, "you've gone a long way toward findin' where 't is. It's just like Ebeneezer to have hid it."

She took down the pictures, which were mainly family portraits, life-size, presented to the master of the house by devoted relatives, and rapidly unframed them. In one of them she found a sealed envelope, which she eagerly tore open.

Inside was a personal communication which, though brief, was very much to the point.

"Dear Cousin Belinda," it read, "I hope you're taking pleasure in your hunt. I have kept my word to you and in this very room, somewhere, is a sum of money which represents my estimate of your worth, as nearly as sordid coin can hope to do. It is all in cash, for greater convenience in handling. I trust you will not spend it all in one store, and that you will, out of your abundance, be generous to the poor. It might be well to use a part of it in making a visit to New York. When you find this, I shall be out in the cemetery all by myself, and very comfortable.

"Yours, Ebeneezer Judson."

"I knowed it," she said to herself, excitedly. "Ebeneezer was a hard man, but he always kep' his word. Dear me! What makes me so trembly!"

She removed all the bedclothes and pounded the pillows and mattress in vain, then turned her attention to the furniture. It was almost one o'clock when Mrs. Dodd finally retired, worn in body and jaded in spirit, but still far from discouraged.

"Ebeneezer must have mistook the room," she said to herself, "but how could he unless his mind was failin'? I've had this now, goin' on ten year."

In the night she dreamed of finding money in the bureau, and got up to see if by chance she had not received mysterious guidance from an unknown source. There was money in the bureau, sure enough, but it was only two worn copper cents wrapped in many thicknesses of old newspaper, and she went unsuspiciously back to bed.

"He's mistook the room," she breathed, drowsily, as she sank into troubled slumber, "an' to-morrer I'll have it changed. It's just as well I've scared them others off, if so be I have."

# XI

## Mrs. Dodd's Third Husband

Insidiously, a single idea took possession of the entire household. Mrs. Smithers kept a spade near at hand and systematically dug, as opportunity offered. Dorothy became accustomed to an odorous lantern which stood near the back door in the daytime and bobbed about among the shrubbery at night.

There was definite method in the madness of Mrs. Smithers, however, for she had once seen the departed Mr. Judson going out to the orchard with a tin box under his arm and her own spade but partially concealed under his long overcoat. When he came back, he was smiling, which was so unusual that she forgot all about the box, and did not observe whether or not he had brought it back with him. Long afterward, however, the incident assumed greater significance.

"If I'd 'ave 'ad the sense to 'ave gone out there the next day," she muttered, "and 'ave seen where 'e 'ad dug, I might be a rich woman now, that's wot I might. 'E was a clever one, 'e was, and 'e's 'id it. The old skinflint wasn't doin' no work, 'e wasn't, and 'e lived on 'ere from year to year, a-payin' 'is bills like a Christian gent, and it stands to reason there's money 'id somewheres. Findin' is keepin', and it's for me to keep my 'ead shut and a sharp lookout. Them Carrs don't suspect nothink."

She was only half right, however. Harlan, lost in his book, was heedless of everything that went on around him, but Mrs. Dodd's reference to the diamond pin, and her own recollection of the money she had found in the bureau drawer, began to work stealthily upon Dorothy's mind, surrounded, as she was, by people who were continually thinking of the same thing.

Then, too, their funds were getting low. There was little to send to the sanitarium now, for eleven people, as students of domestic economics have often observed, eat more than one or two. Dick was also affected by the current financial depression, and at length conceived the idea that Uncle Ebeneezer's worldly goods were somewhere on the premises.

Mrs. Holmes spent a great deal of time in the attic, while the care-free children, utterly beyond control, rioted madly through the house. Dorothy discovered Mr. Perkins, the poet, half-way up the parlour chimney, and sat down to see what he would do when he came out and found her there. He had seemed somewhat embarrassed when he wiped the soot from his face, but had quickly explained that he was writing a poem on chimney-swallows and had come to a point where original research was essential.

Even Elaine, not knowing what she sought, began to investigate, idly enough, the furniture and hangings in her room, and Mrs. Dodd, eagerly seizing opportunities, was forever keen on the scent. Uncle Israel, owing to the poor state of his health, was one of the last to be affected by the surrounding atmosphere, but when he caught the idea, he made up for lost time.

He was up with the chickens, and invariably took a long afternoon nap, so that, during the night, there was bound to be a wakeful interval. Ordinarily, he took a sleeping potion to tide him over till morning, but soon decided that a little mild exercise with some pleasant purpose animating it, would be far better for his nerves.

Mrs. Dodd was awakened one night by the feeling that some one was in her room. A vague, mysterious Presence gradually made itself known. At first she was frightened, then the Presence wheezed, and reassured her. Across the path of moonlight that lay on her floor, Uncle Israel moved cautiously.

He was clad in a piebald dressing-gown which had been so patched with various materials that the original fabric was uncertain. An old-fashioned nightcap was on his head, the tassel bobbing freakishly in the back, and he wore carpet slippers.

Mrs. Dodd sat up in bed, keenly relishing the situation. When he opened a bureau drawer, she screamed out: "What are you looking for?"

Uncle Israel started violently. "Money," he answered, in a shrill whisper, taken altogether by surprise.

"Then," said Mrs. Dodd, kindly, "I'll get right up and help you!"

"Don't, Belinda," pleaded the old man. "You'll wake up everybody. I am a-walkin' in my sleep, I guess. I was a-dreamin' of money that I was to find and give to you, and I suppose that's why I've come to your room. You lay still, Belinda, and don't tell nobody. I am a-goin' right away."

Before she could answer in a way that seemed suitable, he was gone, and the next day he renewed his explanations. "I dunno, Belinda, how I ever come to be a-walkin' in my sleep. I ain't never done such a thing since I was a child, and then only wunst. How dretful it would have been if I had gone into any other room and mebbe have been shot or have scared some young and unprotected female into fits. To think of me, with my untarnished reputation, and at my age, a-doin' such a thing! You don't reckon it was my new pain-killer, do you?"

---

"I don't misdoubt it had sunthin' to do with payin'," returned Mrs. Dodd, greatly pleased with her own poor joke, "an', as you say, it might have been dretful. But I am a friend to you, Israel, an' I don't 'low to make your misfortune public, but, by workin' private, help you overcome it."

"What air you a-layin' out to do?" demanded Uncle Israel, fearfully.

"I ain't rightly made up my mind as yet, Israel," she answered, pleasantly enough, "but I don't intend to have it happen to you again. Sunthin' can surely be done that'll cure you of it."

"Don't, Belinda," wheezed her victim; "I don't think I'll ever have it again."

"Don't you fret about it, Israel, 'cause you ain't goin' to have it no more. I'll attend to it. It 's a most distressin' disease an' must be took early, but I think I know how to fix it."

During her various investigations, she had found a huge bunch of keys beneath a pile of rubbish on the floor of a closet in an unoccupied room. It was altogether possible, as she told herself, that one of these keys should fit the somnambulist's door.

While Uncle Israel was brewing a fresh supply of medicine on the kitchen stove, she found, as she had suspected that one of them did fit, and thereafter, every night, when Uncle Israel had retired, she locked him in, letting him out shortly after seven each morning. When he remonstrated with her, she replied, triumphantly, that it was necessary—otherwise he would never have known that the door was locked.

On her first visit to "town" she made it her business to call upon Lawyer Bradford and inquire as to Mr. Judson's last will and testament. She learned that it did not concern her at all, and was to be probated, in accordance with the dead man's instructions, at the Fall term of court.

"Then, as yet," she said, with a gleam of satisfaction in her small, beady eyes, "they ain't holdin' the house legal. Any of us has the same right to stay as them Carrs."

"That's as you look at it," returned Mr. Bradford, squirming uneasily in his chair.

Try as she might, she could extract no further information, but she at least had a bit of knowledge to work on. She went back, earnestly desiring quiet, that she might study the problem without hindrance, but, unfortunately for her purpose, the interior of the Jack-o'-Lantern resembled pandemonium let loose.

Willie was sliding down the railing part of the time, and at frequent intervals coasting downstairs on Mrs. Smithers's tea tray, vocally expressing his pleasure with each trip. The twins, seated in front of the library door, were pounding furiously on a milk-pan, which had not been empty when they dragged it into the hall, but was now. Mrs. Smithers was singing: "We have our trials here below, Oh, Glory, Hallelujah," and a sickening odour from a fresh concoction of Uncle Israel's permeated the premises. Having irreverently detached the false front from the keys of the melodeon, Mr. Perkins was playing a sad, funereal composition of his own, with all the power of the instrument turned loose on it. Upstairs, Dick was whistling, with shrill and maddening persistence, and Dorothy, quite helpless, sat miserably on the porch with her fingers in her ears.

Harlan burst out of the library, just as Mrs. Dodd came up the walk, his temper not improved by stumbling over the twins and the milk-pan, and above their united wails loudly censured Dorothy for the noise and confusion. "How in the devil do you expect me to work?" he demanded, irritably. "If you can't keep the house quiet, I'll go back to New York!"

Too crushed in spirit to reply, Dorothy said nothing, and Harlan whisked back into the library again, barely escaping Mrs. Dodd.

"Poor child," she said to Dorothy; "you look plum beat out."

"I am," confessed Mrs. Carr, the quick tears coming to her eyes.

"There, there, my dear, rest easy. I reckon this is the first time you've been married, ain't it?"

"Yes," returned Dorothy, forcing a pitiful little smile.

"I thought so. Now, when you're as used to it as I be, you won't take it so hard. You may think men folks is all different, but there's a dretful sameness to 'em after they've been through a marriage ceremony. Marriage is just like findin' a new penny on the walk. When you first see it, it's all shiny an' a'most like gold, an' it tickles you a'most to pieces to think you're gettin' it, but after you've picked it up you see that what you've got is half wild Indian, or mebbe more—I ain't never been in no mint. You may depend upon it, my dear, there's two sides to all of us, an' before marriage, you see the wreath—afterwards a savage.

"I've had seven of 'em," she continued, "an' I know. My father give me a cemetery lot for a weddin' present, with a noble grey marble monumint in it shaped like a octagon—leastways that's what a school-teacher what boarded with us said it was, but I call it a eight-sided piece. I'm speakin' of my first marriage now, my dear. My father never give me no weddin' present but the once. An' I can't never marry again, 'cause there's a husband lyin' now on seven sides of the monumint an' only one place left for me. I was told once that I could have further husbands cremationed an' set around the lot in vases, but I don't take to no such heathenish custom as that.

"So I've got to go through my declinin' years without no suitable companion an' I call it hard, when one's so used to marryin' as what I be."

"If they're all savages," suggested Dorothy, "why did you keep on marrying?"

"Because I hadn't no other way to get my livin' an' I was kinder in the habit of it. There's some little variety, even in savages, an' it's human natur' to keep on a-hopin.' I've had 'em stingy an' generous, drunk an' sober, peaceful an' disturbin'. After the first few times, I learned to take real pleasure out'n their queer notions. When you've learned to enjoy seein' your husband make a fool of himself an' have got enough self-control not to tell him he's doin' it, nor to let him see where your pleasure lies, you've got marryin' down to a fine point.

"The third time, it was, I got a food crank, an' let me tell you right now, my dear, them's the worst kind. A man what's queer about his food is goin' to be queerer about a'most everything else. Give me any man that can eat three square meals a day an' enjoy 'em, an' I'll undertake to live with him peaceful, but I don't go to the altar again with no food crank, if I know it.

"It was partly my own fault, too, as I see later. I'd seen him a-carryin' a passel of health food around in his pocket an' a-nibblin' at it, but I supposed it was because the poor creeter had never had no one to cook proper for him, an' I took a lot of pleasure out of thinkin' how tickled he'd be when I made him one of my chicken pies.

"After we was married, we took a honeymoon to his folks, an' I'll tell you right now, my dear, that if there was more honeymoons took beforehand to each other's folks, there'd be less marryin' done than what there is. They was all a-eatin' hay an' straw an' oats just like the dumb creeters they disdained, an' a-carryin' wheat an' corn around in their pockets to piece out with between greens.

"So the day we got home, never knowin' what I was a-stirrin' up for myself, I turned in an' made a chicken an' oyster pie, an' it couldn't be beat, not if I do say it as shouldn't. The crust was as soft an' flaky an' brown an' crisp at the edges as any I ever turned out, an' the inside was all chicken an' oysters well-nigh smothered in a thick, creamy yellow gravy.

"Well, sir, I brung in that pie, an' I set it on the table, an' I chirped out that dinner was ready, an' he come, an'—my dear! You never saw such goins'-on in all your born days! Considerin' that not eatin' animals makes people's dispositions mild an' pleasant, it was sunthin' terrible, an' me all the time as innercent as a lamb!

"I can't begin to tell you the things my new-made husband said to me. If chickens an' oysters was human, I'll bet they'd have sued him for slander. He said that oysters was 'the scavengers of the sea'—yes'm, them's his very

84

words, an' that chickens was even worse. He went on to tell me how they et worms an' potato bugs an' beetles an' goodness knows what else, an' that he wa'n't goin' to turn the temple of his body into no slaughter-house. He asked me if I desired to eat dead animals, an' when he insisted on an answer, I told him I certainly shouldn't care to eat 'em less'n they *was* dead, and from then on it was worse 'n ever.

"He said that no dead animal was goin' to be interred in the insides of him or his lawful wife, an' he was goin' to see to it. It come out then that he'd never tasted meat an' hadn't rightly sensed what he was missin'.

"Well, my dear, some women would have took the wrong tack an' would have argyfied with him. There's never no use in argyfyin' with a husband, an' never no need to, 'cause if you're set on it, there's all the rest of the world to choose from. When he'd talked himself hoarse an' was beginnin' to calm down again, I took the floor.

"'Say no more,' says I, calm an' collected-like. 'This here is your house an' the things you're accustomed to eatin' can be cooked init, no matter what they be. If I don't know how to put the slops together, I reckon I can learn, not being a plum idjit. If you want baked chicken feed and boiled hay, I'm here to bake 'em and boil 'em for you. All you have to do is to speak once in a polite manner and it'll be done. I must insist on the politeness, howsumever,' says I. 'I don't propose to live with any man what gets the notion a woman ceases to be a lady when she marries him. A creeter that thinks so poor of himself as that ain't fit to be my husband,' says I, 'nor no other decent woman's.'

"At that he apologised some, an' when a husband apologises, my dear, it's the same as if he'd et dirt at your feet. 'The least said the soonest mended,' says I, an' after that, he never had nothin' to complain of.

"But I knowed what his poor, cranky system needed, an' I knowed how to get it into him, especially as he'd never tasted meat in all his life. From that time on, he never saw no meat on our table, nor no chickens, nor sea scavengers, nor nothin', but all day, while he was gone, I was busy with my soup pot, a-makin' condensed extracts of meat for flavourin' vegetables an' sauces an' so on.

"He took mightily to my cookin' an' frequently said he'd never et such exquisite victuals. I'd make cream soups for him, an' in every one, there'd be over a cupful of solid meat jelly, as rich as the juice you find in the pan when you cook a first-class roast of beef. I'd stew potatoes in veal stock, and cook rice slow in water that had had a chicken boiled to rags in it. Once I put a cupful of raw beef juice in a can of tomatoes I was cookin' and he et a'most all of 'em.

"As he kep' on havin' more confidence in me, I kep' on usin' more an' more, an' a-usin' oyster liquor for flavourin' in most everything durin' the R months. Once he found nearly a bushel of clam-shells out behind the house an' wanted to know what they was an' what they was doin' there. I told him the fish man had give 'em to me for a border for my flower beds, which was true. I'd only paid for the clams—there wa'n't nothin' said about the shells—an' the juice from them clams livened up his soup an' vegetables for over a week. There wa'n't no day that he didn't have the vital elements of from one to four pounds of meat put in his food, an' all the time, he was gettin' happier an' healthier an' more peaceful to live with. When he died, he was as mild as a spring lamb with mint sauce on it.

"Now, my dear, some women would have told him what they was doin', either after he got to likin' the cookin' or when he was on his death-bed an' couldn't help himself, but I never did. I own that it took self-control not to do it, but I'd learned my lesson from havin' been married twicet before an' never havin' fit any to speak of. I had to take my pleasure from seein' him eat a bowl of rice that had a whole chicken in it, exceptin' only the bones and fibres of its mortal frame, an' a-lappin' up mebbe a pint of tomato soup that was founded on eight nice pork chops. I'm a-tellin' you all this merely to show you my point. Every day, Henry was makin' a blame fool of himself without knowin' it. He'd prattle by the hour of slaughter-houses an' human cemeteries an' all the time he'd be honin' for his next meal.

"He used to say as how it was dretful wicked to kill the dumb animals for food, an' I allers said that there was nothin' to hinder his buyin' as many as he could afford to an' savin' their lives by pennin' 'em up in the back yard, an' a-feedin' 'em the things they liked best to eat till they died of old age or sunthin'. I told him they was all vegetarians, the same as he was, an' they could live together peaceful an' happy. I even pointed out that it was his duty to do it, an' that if all believers would do the same, the dread slaughter-houses would soon be a thing of the past, but I ain't never seen no food crank yet that's advanced that far in his humanity.

"I never told him a single word about it, nor even hinted it to him, nor told nobody else, though I often felt wicked to think I was keepin' so much pleasure to myself, but my time is comin'.

"When I'm dead an' have gone to heaven, the first thing I'm goin' to do is to hunt up Henry. They say there ain't no marriage nor givin' in marriage up there, but I reckon there's seven men there that'll at least recognise their wife when they see her a-comin' in. I'm goin' to pick up my skirts an' take off my glasses, so's I'll be all ready to skedaddle, for I expect to leave my rheumatiz behind me, my dear, when I go to heaven—leastways, no place will be heaven for me that's got rheumatiz in it—an' then I'm goin' to say: 'Henry, in all he four years you was livin' with me, you was eatin' meat, an' you never knowed it. You're nothin' but a human cemetery.' Oh, my dear, it's worth while dyin' when you know you're goin' to have pleasure like that at the other end!"

# XII

## Her Gift to the World

"I regret, my dear madam," said Lawyer Bradford, twisting uneasily in his chair, "that I can offer you no encouragement whatsoever. The will is clear and explicit in every detail, and there are no grounds for a contest. I am, perhaps, trespassing upon the wishes of my client in giving you this information, but if you are remaining here with the hope of pecuniary profit, you are remaining here unnecessarily."

He rose as though to indicate that the interview was at an end, but Mrs. Holmes was not to be put away in that fashion. Her eyes were blazing and her weak chin trembled with anger.

"Do you mean to tell me," she demanded, "that Ebeneezer voluntarily died without making some sort of provision for me and my helpless little children?"

"Your distinguished relation," answered Mr. Bradford, slowly, "certainly died voluntarily. He announced the date of his death some weeks before it actually occurred, and superintended the making of his own coffin. He wrote out minute directions for his obsequies, had his grave dug, and his shroud made, burned his papers, rearranged his books, made his will—and was found dead in his bed on the morning of the day set for his departure. A methodical person," muttered the old man, half to himself; "a most methodical and systematic person."

Mrs. Holmes shuddered. She was not ordinarily a superstitious woman, but there was something uncanny in this open partnership with Death.

"There was a diamond pin," she suggested, moodily, "worth, I should think, some fifteen or sixteen hundred dollars. Ebeneezer gave it to dear Rebecca on their wedding day, and she always said it was to be mine. Have you any idea where it is?"

Mr. Bradford fidgeted. "If it was intended for you," he said, finally, "it will be given to you at the proper time, or you will be directed to its location. Mrs. Judson died, did she not, about three weeks after their marriage?"

"Yes," snapped Mrs. Holmes, readily perceiving the line of his thought, "and I saw her twice in those three weeks. Both times she spoke of the pin, which she wore constantly, and said that if anything happened to her, she wanted me to have it, but that old miser hung on to it."

"Madam," said Mr. Bradford, a faint flush mounting to his temples as he opened the office door, "you are speaking of my Colonel, under whom I served in the war. He was my best friend, and though he is dead, it is still my privilege to protect him. I bid you good afternoon!"

She did not perceive until long afterward that she had practically been ejected from the legal presence. Even then, she was so intent upon the point at issue that she was not offended, as at another time she certainly would have been.

"He's lying," she said to herself, "they're all lying. There's money hidden in that house, and I know it, and what's more, I'm going to have it!"

She had searched her own rooms on the night of her arrival, but found nothing, and the attic, so far, had yielded her naught save discouragement and dust. "To think," she continued, mentally, "that after two of my children were born here and named for them, that we are left in this way! I call it a shame, a disgrace, an outrage!"

Her anger swiftly cooled, however, as she went into the house, and her fond sight rested upon her darlings. Willie had a ball and had already broken two of the front windows. The small Rebecca was under the sofa, tempering the pleasure of life for Claudius Tiberius, while young Ebeneezer, having found a knife somewhere, was diligently scratching the melodeon.

"Just look," said Mrs. Holmes, in delighted awe, as Dorothy entered the room. "Don't make any noise, or you will disturb Ebbie. He is such a sensitive child that the sound of a strange voice will upset him. Did you ever see anything like those figures he is drawing on the melodeon? I believe he's going to be an artist!"

Crushed as she was in spirit by her uncongenial surroundings, Dorothy still had enough temper left to be furiously angry. In these latter days, however, she had gained largely in self-control, and now only bit her lips without answering.

But Mrs. Holmes would not have heard her, even if she had replied. A sudden yowl from the distressed Claudius impelled Dorothy to move the sofa and rescue him.

"How cruel you are!" commented Mrs. Holmes. "The idea of taking Rebbie's plaything away from her! Give it back this instant!"

Mrs. Carr put the cat out and returned with a defiant expression on her face, which roused Mrs. Holmes to action. "Willie," she commanded, "go out and get the kitty for your little sister. There, there, Rebbie, darling, don't cry any more! Brother has gone to get the kitty. Don't cry!"

But "brother" had not gone. "Chase it yourself," he remarked, coolly. "I'm going out to the barn."

"Dear Willie's individuality is developing every day," Mrs. Holmes went on, smoothly. "There, there, Rebbie, don't cry any more. Go and tell Mrs. Smithers to give you a big piece of bread with lots of butter and jam on it. Tell her mamma said so. Run along, that's a nice little girl."

Rude squares, triangles, and circles appeared as by magic on the shining surface of the melodeon, the young artist being not at all disturbed by the confusion about him.

"I am blessed in my children," Mrs. Holmes went on, happily. "I often wonder what I have done that I should have so perfect a boy as Willie for my very own. Everybody admires him so that I dwell in constant fear of kidnappers."

"I wouldn't worry," said Dorothy, with ill-concealed sarcasm. "Anybody who took him would bring him back inside of two hours."

"I try to think so," returned the mother, with a deep sigh. "Willie's indomitable will is my deepest comfort. He gets it from my side of the family. None of the children take after their father at all. Ebbie was a little like his father's folks at first, but I soon got it out of him and made him altogether like my people. I do not think anybody could keep Willie away from me except by superior physical force. He absolutely adores his mother, as my other children do. You never saw such beautiful sentiment as they have. The other day, now, when I went away and left Rebbie alone in my apartment, she took down my best hat and put it on. The poor little thing wanted to be near her mother. Is it not touching?"

"It is indeed," Dorothy assented, dryly.

"My children have never been punished," continued Mrs. Holmes, now auspiciously launched upon her favourite theme. "It has never been necessary. I rule them entirely through love, and they are so accustomed to my methods that they bitterly resent any interference by outsiders. Why, just before we came here, Ebbie, young as he is, put out the left eye of a woman who tried to take his dog away from him. He did it with his little fist and with apparently no effort at all. Is it not wonderful to see such strength and power of direction in one so young? The woman was in the hospital when we came away, and I trust by this time, she has learned not to interfere with Ebbie. No one is allowed to interfere with my children."

"Apparently not," remarked Mrs. Carr, somewhat cynically.

"It is beautiful to be a mother—the most beautiful thing on earth! Just think how much I have done for the world!" Her sallow face glowed with the conscious virtue bestowed by one of the animal functions upon those who have performed it.

"In what way?" queried Mrs. Carr, wholly missing the point.

"Why, in raising Willie and Ebbie and Rebbie! No public service can for a moment be compared with that! All other things sink into insignificance beside the glorious gift of maternity. Look at Willie—a form that a sculptor might dream of for a lifetime and never hope to imitate—a head that already has inspired great artists! The gentleman who took Willie's last tintype said that he had never seen such perfect lines, and insisted on taking several for fear something should happen to Willie. He wanted to keep some of them for himself—it was pathetic, the way he pleaded, but I made him sell me all of them. Willie is mine and I have the first right to his tintypes. And a lady once painted Willie at his play in black and white and sent it to one of the popular weeklies. I have no doubt they gave her a fortune for it, but it never occurred to her to give us anything more than one copy of the paper."

"Which paper was it?"

"One of the so-called comic weeklies. You know they publish superb artistic things. I think they are doing a wonderful work in educating the masses to a true appreciation of art. One of the wonderful parts of it was that Willie knew all about it and was not in the least conceited. Any other child would have been set up at being a model for a great artist, but Willie was not affected at all. He has so much character!"

At this point the small Rebecca entered, dragging her doll by one arm, and munching a thick slice of bread, thinly coated with molasses.

"I distinctly said jam," remarked Mrs. Holmes. "Servants are so heedless. I do not know that molasses is good for Rebbie. What would you think, Mrs. Carr?"

"I don't think it will hurt her if she doesn't get too much of it."

"There's no danger of her getting too much of it. Mrs. Smithers is too stingy for that. Why, only yesterday, Willie told me that she refused to let him dip his dry bread in the cream, and gave him a cup of plain milk instead. Willie knows when his system needs cream and I want him to have all the nourishment he can get. The idea that she should think she knew more about it than Willie! She was properly punished for it, however. I myself saw Willie throw a stick of stove wood at her and hit her foolish head with it. I think Willie is going to be a soldier, a commander of an army. He has so much executive ability and never misses what he aims at.

"Rebbie, don't chew on that side, darling; remember your loose tooth is there. Mamma doesn't want it to come out."

"Why?" asked Dorothy, with a gleam of interest.

"Because I can't bear to have her little baby teeth come out and make her grow up! I want to keep her just as she is. I have all my children's teeth, and some day I am going to have them set into a beautiful bracelet. Look at that! How generous and unselfish of Rebbie! She is trying to share her bread with her doll. I believe Rebbie is going to be a philanthropist, or a college-settlement worker. See, she is trying to give the doll the molasses—the very best part of it. Did you ever see such a beautiful spirit in one so young?"

Before Mrs. Carr could answer, young Ebeneezer had finished his wood carving and had grabbed his protesting twin by the hair.

"There, there, Rebbie," soothed the mother, "don't cry. Brother was only loving little sister. Be careful, Ebbie. You can take hold of sister's hair, but not too hard. They love each other so," she went on. "Ebbie is really sentimental about Rebbie. He loves to touch and stroke her glorious blonde hair. Did you ever see such hair as Rebbie's?"

It came into Mrs. Carr's mind that "Rebbie's" hair looked more like a plate of cold-slaw than anything else, but she was too wise to put the thought into words.

Willie slid down the railing and landed in the hall with a loud whoop of glee. "How beautiful to hear the sounds of childish mirth," said Mrs. Holmes. "How——"

From upstairs came a cry of "Help! Help!"

Muffled though the voice was, it plainly issued from Uncle Israel's room, and under the impression that the bath cabinet had finally set the house on fire, Mrs. Carr ran hastily upstairs, followed closely by Mrs. Holmes, who was flanked at the rear by the grinning Willie and the interested twins.

From a confused heap of bedding, Uncle Israel's scarlet ankles waved frantically. "Help! Help!" he cried again, his voice being almost wholly deadened by the pillows, which had fallen on him after the collapse.

Dorothy helped the trembling old man to his feet. He took a copious draught from the pain-killer, then sat down on his trunk, much perturbed.

Investigation proved that the bed cord had been cut in a dozen places by some one working underneath, and that the entire structure had instantly caved in when Uncle Israel had crept up to the summit of his bed and lain down to take his afternoon nap. When questioned, Willie proudly admitted that he had done it.

"Go down and ask Mrs. Smithers for the clothes-line," commanded Dorothy, sternly.

"I won't," said Willie, smartly, putting his hands in his pockets.

"You had better go yourself, Mrs. Carr," suggested Mrs. Holmes. "Willie is tired. He has played hard all day and needs rest. He must not on any account over-exert himself, and, besides, I never allow any one else to send my children on errands. They obey me and me alone."

"Go yourself," said Willie, having gathered encouragement from the maternal source.

"I'll go," wheezed Uncle Israel. "I can't sleep in no other bed. Ebeneezer's beds is all terrible drafty, and I took two colds at once sleepin' in one of 'em when I knowed better 'n to try it." He tottered out of the room, the very picture of wretchedness.

"Was it not clever of Willie?" whispered Mrs. Holmes, admiringly, to Dorothy. "So much ingenuity—such a fine sense of humor!"

"If he were my child," snapped Dorothy, at last losing her admirable control of a tempestuous temper, "he'd be soundly thrashed at least three times a week!"

"I do not doubt it," replied Mrs. Holmes, contemptuously. "These married old maids, who have no children of their own, are always wholly out of sympathy with a child's nature."

"When I was young," retorted Mrs. Carr, "children were not allowed to rule the entire household. There was a current superstition to the effect that older people had some rights."

"And yet," Mrs. Holmes continued, meditatively, "as the editor of *The Ladies' Own* so pertinently asks, what is a house for if not to bring up a child in? The purpose of architecture is defeated, where there are no children."

Uncle Israel, accompanied by Dick, hobbled into the room with the clothes-line. Mrs. Holmes discreetly retired, followed by her offspring, and, late in the afternoon, when Dorothy and Dick were well-nigh fagged out, the structure was in place again. Tremulously the exhausted owner lay down upon it, and asked that his supper be sent to his room.

By skilful manœuvring with Mrs. Smithers, Dick compelled the proud-spirited Willie to take up Uncle Israel's tray and wait for it. "I'll tell my mother," whimpered the sorrowful one.

"I hope you will," replied Dick, significantly; but for some reason of his own, Willie neglected to mention it.

At dinner-time, Mr. Perkins drew a rolled manuscript, tied with a black ribbon, from his breast pocket, and, without preliminary, proceeded to read as follows:

TO THE MEMORY OF EBENEEZER JUDSON


A face we loved has vanished,


A voice we adored is now still,

There is no longer any music

In the tinkling rill.

His hat is empty of his head,

His snuff-box has no sneezer,

His cane is idle in the hall

For gone is Ebeneezer.

Within the house we miss him,

Let fall the sorrowing tear,

Yet shall we gather as was our wont

Year after sunny year.

He took such joy in all his friends

That he would have it so;

He left his house to relatives

But none of us need go.

In fact, we're all related,

Sister, friend, and brother;

And in this hour of our grief

We must console each other.

He would not like to have us sad,

Our smiles were once his pleasure

And though we cannot smile at him,

His memory is our treasure.

When he had finished, there was a solemn silence, which was at last relieved by Mrs. Dodd. "Poetry broke out in my first husband's family," she said, "but with sulphur an' molasses an' quinine an' plenty of wet-sheet packs it was finally cured."

"You do not understand," said the poet, indulgently. "Your aura is not harmonious with mine."

---

"Your—what?" demanded Mrs. Dodd, pricking up her ears.

"My aura," explained Mr. Perkins, flushing faintly. "Each individuality gives out a spiritual vapour, like a cloud, which surrounds one. These are all in different colours, and the colours change with the thoughts we think. Black and purple are the gloomy, morose colours; deep blue and the paler shades show a sombre outlook on life; green is more cheerful, though still serious; yellow and orange show ambition and envy, and red and white are emblematic of all the virtues—red of the noble, martial qualities of man and white of the angelic disposition of woman," he concluded, with a meaning glance at Elaine, who had been much interested all along.

"What perfectly lovely ideas," she said, in a tone which made Dick's blood boil. "Are they original with you, Mr. Perkins?"

The poet cleared his throat. "I cannot say that they are wholly original with me," he admitted, reluctantly, "though of course I have modified and amplified them to accord with my own individuality. They are doing wonderful things now in the psychological laboratories. They have a system of tubes so finely constructed that by breathing into one of them a person's mental state is actually expressed. An angry person, breathing into one of these finely organised tubes, makes a decided change in the colour of the vapour."

"Humph!" snorted Mrs. Dodd, pushing back her chair briskly. "I've been married seven times, an' I never had to breathe into no tube to let any of my husbands know when I was mad!"

The poet crimsoned, but otherwise ignored the comment. "If you will come into the parlour just as twilight is falling," he said to the others, "I will gladly recite my ode on Spring."

Subdued thanks came from the company, though Harlan excused himself on the score of his work, and Mrs. Holmes was obliged to put the twins to bed. When twilight fell, no one was at the rendezvous but Elaine and the poet.

"It is just as well," he said, in a low tone. "There are several under dear Uncle Ebeneezer's roof who are afflicted with an inharmonious aura. With yours only am I in full accord. It is a great pleasure to an artist to feel such beautiful sympathy with his work. Shall I say it now?"

"If you will," murmured Elaine, deeply honoured by acquaintance with a real poet.

Mr. Perkins drew his chair close to hers, leaned over with an air of loving confidence, and began:

Spring, oh Spring, dear, gentle Spring,

My poet's garland do I bring

To lay upon thy shining hair

Where rests a wreath of flowers so fair.

There is a music in the brook

Which answers to thy tender look

And in thy eyes there is a spell

Of soft enchantment too sweet to tell.

My heart to thine shall ever turn

For thou hast made my soul to burn

With rapture far beyond——

Elaine screamed, and in a twinkling was on her chair with her skirts gathered about her. It was only Claudius Tiberius, dressed in Rebecca's doll's clothes, scooting madly toward the front door, but it served effectually to break up the entertainment.

# XIII

## A Sensitive Soul

Uncle Israel was securely locked in for the night, and was correspondingly restless. He felt like a caged animal, and sleep, though earnestly wooed, failed to come to his relief. A powerful draught of his usual sleeping potion had been like so much water, as far as effect was concerned.

At length he got up, his lifelong habit of cautious movement asserting itself even here, and with tremulous, withered hands, lighted his candle. Then he put on his piebald dressing-gown and his carpet slippers, and sat on the declivity of his bed, blinking at the light, as wide awake as any owl.

Presently it came to him that he had not as yet made a thorough search of his own apartment, so he began at the foundation, so to speak, and crawled painfully over the carpet, paying special attention to the edges. Next, he fingered the baseboards carefully, rapping here and there, as though he expected some significant sound to penetrate his deafness. Rising, he went over the wall systematically, and at length, with the aid of a chair, reached up to the picture-moulding. He had gone nearly around the room, without any definite idea of what he was searching for, when his questioning fingers touched a small, metallic object.

A smile of childlike pleasure transfigured Uncle Israel's wizened old face. Trembling, he slipped down from the chair, falling over the bath cabinet in his descent, and tried the key in the lock. It fitted, and the old man fairly chuckled.

"Wait till I tell Belinda," he muttered, delightedly. Then a crafty second thought suggested that it might be wiser to keep "Belinda" in the dark, lest she might in some way gain possession of the duplicate key.

"Lor'," he thought, "but how I pity them husbands of her'n. Bet their graves felt good when they got into 'em, the hull seven graves. What with sneerin' at medicines and things a person eats, it must have been awful, not to mention stealin' of keys and a-lockin' 'em in nights. S'pose the house had got afire, where'd I be now?" Grasping his treasure closely, Uncle Israel blew out his candle and tottered to bed, thereafter sleeping the sleep of the just.

Mrs. Dodd detected subdued animation in his demeanour when he appeared at breakfast the following morning, and wondered what had occurred.

"You look 's if sunthin' pleasant had happened, Israel," she began in a sprightly manner.

"Sunthin' pleasant has happened," he returned, applying himself to his imitation coffee with renewed vigour. "I disremember when I've felt so good about anythin' before."

"Something pleasant happens every day," put in Elaine. The country air had made roses bloom on her pale cheeks. Her blue eyes had new light in them, and her golden hair fairly shone. She was far more beautiful than the sad, frail young woman who had come to the Jack-o'-Lantern not so many weeks before.

"How optimistic you are!" sighed Mr. Perkins, who was eating Mrs. Smithers's crisp, hot rolls with a very unpoetic appetite. "To me, the world grows worse every day. It is only a few noble souls devoted to the Ideal and holding their heads steadfastly above the mire of commercialism that keep our so-called civilisation from becoming an absolute hotbed of greed—yes, a hotbed of greed," he repeated, the words sounding unexpectedly well.

"Your aura seems to have a purple tinge this morning," commented Dorothy, slyly.

"What's a aura, ma?" demanded Willie, with an unusual thirst for knowledge.

"Something that goes with a soft person, Willie, dear," responded Mrs. Holmes, quite audibly. "You know there are some people who have no backbone at all, like the jelly-fish we saw at the seashore the year before dear papa died."

"I've knowed folks," continued Mrs. Dodd, taking up the wandering thread of the discourse, "what was so soft when they was little that their mas had to carry 'em around in a pail for fear they'd slop over and spile the carpet."

"And when they grew up, too," Dick ventured.

"Some people," said Harlan, in a polite attempt to change the conversation, "never grow up at all. Their minds remain at a fixed point. We all know them."

"Yes," sighed Mrs. Dodd, looking straight at the poet, "we all know them."

At this juncture the sensitive Mr. Perkins rose and begged to be excused. It was the small Ebeneezer who observed that he took a buttered roll with him, and gratuitously gave the information to the rest of the company.

Elaine flushed painfully, and presently excused herself, following the crestfallen Mr. Perkins to the orchard, where, entirely unsuspected by the others, they had a trysting-place. At intervals, they met, safely screened by the friendly trees, and communed upon the old, idyllic subject of poetry, especially as represented by the unpublished works of Harold Vernon Perkins.

"I cannot tell you, Mr. Perkins," Elaine began, "how deeply I appreciate your fine, uncommercial attitude. As you say, the world is sordid, and it needs men like you."

The soulful one ran his long, bony fingers through his mane of auburn hair, and assented with a pleased grunt. "There are few, Miss St. Clair," he said, "who have your fine discernment. It is almost ideal."

"Yet it seems too bad," she went on, "that the world-wide appreciation of your artistic devotion should not take some tangible form. Dollars may be vulgar and sordid, as you say, but still, in our primitive era, they are our only expression of value. I have even heard it said," she went on, rapidly, "that the amount of wealth honestly acquired by any individual was, after all, only the measure of his usefulness to his race."

"Miss St. Clair!" exclaimed the poet, deeply shocked; "do I understand that you are actually advising me to sell a poem?"

"Far from it, Mr. Perkins," Elaine reassured him. "I was only thinking that by having your work printed in a volume, or perhaps in the pages of a magazine, you could reach a wider audience, and thus accomplish your ideal of uplifting the multitude."

"I am pained," breathed the poet; "inexpressibly pained."

"Then I am sorry," answered Elaine. "I was only trying to help."

"To think," continued Mr. Perkins, bitterly, "of the soiled fingers of a labouring man, a printer, actually touching these fancies that even I hesitate to pen! Once I saw the fair white page of a book that had been through that painful experience. You never would have known it, my dear Miss St. Clair—it was actually filthy!"

"I see," murmured Elaine, duly impressed, "but are there not more favourable conditions?"

"I have thought there might be," returned the poet, after a significant silence, "indeed, I have prayed there might be. In some little nook among the pines, where the brook for ever sings and the petals of the apple blossoms glide away to fairyland upon its shining surface, while butterflies float lazily here and there, if reverent hands might put the flowering of my genius into a modest little book—I should be tempted, yes, sorely tempted."

"Dear Mr. Perkins," cried Elaine, ecstatically clapping her hands, "how perfectly glorious that would be! To think how much sweetness and beauty would go into the book, if that were done!"

"Additionally," corrected Mr. Perkins, with a slight flush.

"Yes, of course I mean additionally. One could smell the apple blossoms through the printed page. Oh, Mr. Perkins, if I only had the means, how gladly would I devote my all to this wonderful, uplifting work!"

The poet glanced around furtively, then drew closer to Elaine. "I may tell you," he murmured, "in strict confidence, something which my lips have never breathed before, with the assurance that it will be as though unsaid, may I not?"

"Indeed you may!"

"Then," whispered Mr. Perkins, "I am living in that hope. My dear Uncle Ebeneezer, though now departed, was a distinguished patron of the arts. Many a time have I read him my work, assured of his deep, though unexpressed sympathy, and, lulled by the rhythm of our spoken speech, he has passed without a jar from my dreamland to his own. I know he would never speak of it to any one—dear Uncle Ebeneezer was too finely grained for that—but still I feel assured that somewhere within the walls of that sorely afflicted house, a sum of—of money—has been placed, in the hope that I might find it and carry out this beautiful work."

"Have you hunted?" demanded Elaine, her eyes wide with wonder.

"No—not hunted. I beg you, do not use so coarse a word. It jars upon my poet's soul with almost physical pain."

"I beg your pardon," returned Elaine, "but——"

"Sometimes," interrupted the poet, in a low tone, "when I have felt especially near to Uncle Ebeneezer's spirit, I have barely glanced in secret places where I have felt he might expect me to look for it, but, so far, I have been wholly unsuccessful, though I know that I plainly read his thought."

"Some word—some clue—did he give you none?"

"None whatever, except that once or twice he said that he would see that I was suitably provided for. He intimated that he intended me to have a sum apportioned to my deserts."

"Which would be a generous one; but now—Oh, Mr. Perkins, how can I help you?"

"You have never suspected, have you," asked Mr. Perkins, colouring to his temples, "that the room you now occupy might once have been my own? Have no poet's dreams, lingering in the untenanted spaces, claimed your beauteous spirit in sleep?"

"Oh, Mr. Perkins, have I your room? I will so gladly give it up—I——"

The poet raised his hand. "No. The place where you have walked is holy ground. Not for the world would I dispossess you, but——"

A meaning look did the rest. "I see," said Elaine, quickly guessing his thought, "you want to hunt in my room. Oh, Mr. Perkins, I have thoughtlessly pained you again. Can you ever forgive me?"

"My thoughts," breathed Mr. Perkins, "are perhaps too finely phrased for modern speech. I would not trespass upon the place you have made your own, but——"

There was a brief silence, then Elaine understood. "I see," she said, submissively, "I will hunt myself. I mean, I will glance about in the hope that the spirit of Uncle Ebeneezer may make plain to me what you seek. And——"

"And," interjected the poet, quite practical for the moment, "whatever you find is mine, for it was once my room. It is only on account of Uncle Ebeneezer's fine nature and his constant devotion to the Ideal that he did not give it to me direct. He knew it would pain me if he did so. You will remember?"

"I will remember. You need not fear to trust me."

"Then let us shake hands upon our compact." For a moment, Elaine's warm, rosy hand rested in the clammy, nerveless palm of Harold Vernon Perkins. "Last night," he sighed, "I could not sleep. I was distressed by noises which appeared to emanate from the apartment of Mr. Skiles. Did you hear nothing?"

"Nothing," returned Elaine; "I sleep very soundly."

"The privilege of unpoetic souls," commented Mr. Perkins. "But, as usual, my restlessness was not without definite and beautiful result. In the still watches of the night, I achieved a—poem."

"Read it," cried Elaine, rapturously. "Oh, if I might hear it!"

Thus encouraged, Mr. Perkins drew a roll from his breast pocket. A fresh blue ribbon held it in cylindrical form, and the drooping ends waved in careless, artistic fashion.

"As you might expect, if you knew about such things," he began, clearing his throat, and all unconscious of the rapid approach of Mr. Chester, "it is upon sleep. It is done in the sonnet form, a very beautiful measure which I have made my own. I will read it now.


"SONNET ON SLEEP


"O Sleep, that fillst the human breast with peace,


When night's dim curtains swing from out the West,

---

103

In what way, in what manner, could we rest

Were thy beneficent offices to cease?

O Sleep, thou art indeed the snowy fleece

Upon Day's lamb. A welcome guest

That comest alike to palace and to nest

And givest the cares of life a glad release.

O Sleep, I beg thee, rest upon my eyes,

For I am weary, worn, and sad,—indeed,

Of thy great mercies have I piteous need

So come and lead me off to Paradise."

His voice broke at the end, not so much from the intrinsic beauty of the lines as from perceiving Mr. Chester close at hand, grinning like the fabled pussy-cat of Cheshire, except that he did not fade away, leaving only the grin.
Elaine felt the alien presence and looked around. Woman-like, she quickly grasped the situation.

"I have been having a rare treat, Mr. Chester," she said, in her smoothest tones. "Mr. Perkins has very kindly been reading to me his beautiful *Sonnet on Sleep*, composed during a period of wakefulness last night. Did you hear it? Is it not a most unusual sonnet?"

"It is, indeed," answered Dick, dryly. "I never before had the privilege of hearing one that contained only twelve lines. Dante and Petrarch and Shakespeare and all those other ducks put fourteen lines in every blamed sonnet, for good measure."

Hurt to the quick, the sensitive poet walked away.

"How can you speak so!" cried Elaine, angrily. "Is not Mr. Perkins privileged to create a form?"

"To create a form, yes," returned Dick, easily, "but not to monkey with an old one. There's a difference."

Elaine would have followed the injured one had not Dick interfered. He caught her hand quickly, a new and unaccountable lump in his throat suddenly choking his utterance. "I say, Elaine," he said, huskily, "you're not thinking of hooking up with that red-furred lobster, are you?"

"I do not know," responded Elaine, with icy dignity, "what your uncouth language may mean, but I tolerate no interference whatever with my personal affairs." In a moment she was gone, and Dick watched the slender, pink-clad figure returning to the house with ill-concealed emotion.

All Summer, so far, he and Elaine had been good friends. They had laughed and joked and worked together in a care-free, happy-go-lucky fashion. The arrival of Mr. Perkins and his sudden admiration of Elaine had crystallised the situation. Dick knew now what caused the violent antics of his heart—a peaceful and well-behaved organ which had never before been so disturbed by a woman.

"I've got it," said Dick, to himself, deeply shamed. "Moonlight, poetry, mit-holding, and all the rest of it. Never having had it before, it's going hard with me. Why in the devil wasn't I taught to write doggerel when I was in college? A fellow don't stand any show nowadays unless he's a pocket edition of Byron."

He went on through the orchard at a run, instinctively healing a troubled mind by wearying the body. At the outer edge of it, he paused.

Suspended by a singularly strong bit of twine, a small, grinning skull hung from the lower branch of an apple tree, far out on the limb. "Cat's skull," thought Dick. "Wonder who hung it up there?"

He lingered, idly, for a moment or two, then observed that a small patch of grass directly underneath it was of that season's growth. His curiosity fully awake, he determined to dig a bit, though he had dug fruitlessly in many places since he came to the Jack-o'-Lantern.

"Uncle couldn't do anything conventional," he said to himself, "and I'm pretty sure he wouldn't want any of his relations to have his money. Here goes, just for luck!"

He went back to the barn for the spade, which already had fresh earth on it—the evidence of an early morning excavation privately made by Mrs. Smithers in a spot where she had dreamed gold was hidden. He went off to the orchard with it, whistling, his progress being furtively watched with great interest by the sour-faced handmaiden in the kitchen.

Back in the orchard again, he worked feverishly, possessed by a pleasant thrill of excitement, somewhat similar to that conceivably enlivening the humdrum existence of Captain Kidd. Dick was far from surprised when his spade struck something hard, and, his hands trembling with eagerness, he lifted out a tin box of the kind commonly used for private papers.

It was locked, but a twist of his muscular hands sufficed to break it open. Then he saw that it was a spring lock, and that, with grim, characteristic humour, Uncle Ebeneezer had placed the key inside the box. There were papers there—and money, the coins and bills being loosely scattered about, and the papers firmly sealed in an envelope addressed "To Whom it May Concern."

Dick counted the coins and smoothed out the bills, more puzzled than he had ever been in his life. He was tempted to open the envelope, but refrained, not at all sure that he was among those whom it concerned. For the space of half an hour he stood there, frowning, then he laughed.

"I'll just put it back," he said to himself. "It's not for me to monkey with Uncle Ebeneezer's purposes."

He buried the box in its old place, and even cut a bit of sod from a distant part of the orchard to hide the traces of his work. When all was smooth again, he went back to the barn, swinging the spade carelessly but no longer whistling.

"The old devil," he muttered, with keen appreciation. "The wise old devil!"

# XIV

# Mrs. Dodd's Fifth Fate

*Morning lay fair upon the land, and yet the Lady Elaine was weary. Like a drooping lily she swayed in her saddle, sick at heart and cast down. Earnestly her company of gallant knights strove to cheer her, but in vain. Even the merry quips of the fool in motley, who still rode at her side, brought no smile to her beautiful face.*

*Presently, he became silent, his heart deeply troubled because of her. An hour passed so, and no word was spoken, then, timidly enough, he ventured another jest.*

*The Lady Elaine turned. "Say no more, fool," she commanded, "but get out thy writing tablet and compose me a poem. I would fain hear something sad and tender in place of this endless folly."*

*Le Jongleur bowed. "And the subject, Princess?"*

*Elaine laughed bitterly. "Myself," she cried. "Why not? Myself, Elaine, and this foolish quest of mine!"*

*Then, for a space, there was silence upon the road, since the fool, with his writing tablet, had dropped back to the rear of the company, and the gallant knights, perceiving the mood of their mistress, spoke not.*

*At noon, when the white sun trembled at the zenith, Le Jongleur urged his donkey forward, and presented to Elaine a glorious rose which he had found blooming at the wayside.*

*"The poem is finished, your highness," he breathed, doffing his cap, "but 'tis all unworthy, so I bring thee this rose also, that something in my offering may of a certainty be sweet."*

*He would have put the scroll into her hand, but she swerved her palfrey aside. "Read it," she said, impatiently; "I have no mind to try my wits with thy poor scrawls."*

*So, with his voice trembling, and overwhelmed with self-consciousness, the fool read as follows:*

The vineyards, purple with their bloom,

Elaine, hast thou forgotten?

The maidens in thy lonely room,

Thy tapestry on silent loom—

But hush! Where is Elaine?

Elaine, hast thou forgotten?

Thy castle in the valley lies,

Elaine, hast thou forgotten?

Where swift the homing swallow flies

And in the sunset daylight dies—

But hush! Where is Elaine?

Elaine, hast thou forgotten?

Night comes at last on dreamy wings,

Elaine, hast thou forgotten?

'Mid gleaming clouds the pale moon swings,

Thy taper light a faint star brings,

But hush! Where is Elaine?

Elaine, hast thou forgotten?

Harlan had never written any poetry before, but it had always seemed easy. Now, as he read the verses over again, he was tremendously satisfied with his achievement. Unconsciously, he had modelled it upon an exquisite little bit by some one else, which had once been reprinted beneath a "story" of his own when he was on the paper. He read it aloud, to see how it sounded, and was more pleased than ever with the swing of the verse and the music of the words. "It's pretty close to art," he said to himself, "if it isn't the real thing."

Just then the luncheon bell rang, and he went out to the midday "gab-fest," as he inwardly characterised it. The meal proceeded to dessert without any unusual disturbance, then the diminutive Ebeneezer threw the remnants of his cup of milk into his mother's face, and was carried off, howling, to be spanked. Like many other mothers, Mrs. Holmes resented her children's conduct when it incommoded her, but not otherwise, and though milk baths are said to be fine for the complexion, she was not altogether pleased with the manner of application.

Amid the vocal pyrotechnics from the Holmes apartments, Harlan escaped into the library, but his poem was gone. He searched for it vainly, then sat down to write it over before he should forget it. This done, he went on with Elaine and her adventures, and presently forgot all about the lost page.

"Don't that do your heart good?" inquired Mrs. Dodd, of Dorothy, inclining her head toward Mrs. Holmes's door.

"Be it ever so humble," sang Dick, strolling out of the room, "there's no place like Holmes's."

Mrs. Carr admitted that her ears were not yet so calloused but that the sound gave her distinct pleasure.

"If that there little limb of Satan had have throwed his milk in anybody else's face," went on Mrs. Dodd, "all she'd have said would have been: 'Ebbie, don't spill your nice milk. That's naughty.'"

Her imitation of the fond mother's tone and manner was so wickedly exact that Dorothy laughed heartily. The others had fled to a more quiet spot, except Willie and Rebecca, who were fighting for a place at the keyhole of their mother's door. Finally, Willie gained possession of the keyhole, and the ingenious Rebecca, lying flat on her small stomach, peered under the door, and obtained a pleasing view of what was going on inside.

"Listen at that!" cried Mrs. Dodd, her countenance fairly beaming with innocent pleasure. "I'm gettin' most as much good out of it as I would from goin' to the circus. Reckon it's a slipper, for it sounds just like little Jimmie Young's weepin' did the night I come home from my fifth honeymoon.

"That's the only time," she went on, reminiscently, "as I was ever a step-ma to children what wasn't growed up. You'd think a woman as had been married four times afore would have knowed better 'n to get her fool head into a noose like that, but there seems to be only one way for folks to learn things, an' that's by their own experience. If we could only use other folks' experience, this here world would be heaven in about three generations, but we're so constituted that we never believe fire 'll burn till we poke our own fingers into it to see. Other folks' scars don't go no ways at all toward convincin' us.

"You read lots of novels about the sorrers of step-children, but I ain't never come up with no epic as yet portrayin' the sufferin's of a step-ma. If I had a talent like your husband's got, I'll be blest if I wouldn't do it. What I went through with them children aged me ten years in less 'n three.

"It was like this," she prattled on. "I'd never seen a one of 'em, they livin' far away from their pa, as was necessary if their pa was to get any peace an' happiness out 'n life, an' that lyin' creeter I married told me there was only three. My dear, there was eight, an' sixteen ordinary young ones couldn't have been no worse.

"Our courtin' was done mainly in the cemetery. I'd just laid my fourth away in his proper place an' had the letterin' all cut nice on his side of the monumint, an' I was doin' the plantin' on the grave when I met my fate—my fifth fate, I'm speakin' of now. I allers aimed to do right by my husbands when they was dead no less 'n when they was livin', an' I allers planted each one's favourite flower on his last restin'-place, an' planted it thick, so 's when the last trump sounded an' they all riz up, there wouldn't be no one of 'em that could accuse me of bein' partial.

"Some of the flowers was funny for a graveyard. One of 'em loved sunflowers, an' when blossomin'-time come, you could see a spot of light in my lot clear from the gate when you went in, an' on sunny days even from quite a piece outside.

"Geraniums was on the next grave, red an' pink together, as William loved to see 'em, an' most fittin' an' appropriate. He was a queer-lookin' man, William was, all bald except for a little fringe of red hair around his head, an' his bald spot gettin' as pink as anythin' when he got mad. I never could abide red an' pink together, so I did my best not to rile him; but la sakes, my dear, red-haired folks is that touchy that you never can tell what's goin' to rile 'em an' what ain't. Some innercent little remark is as likely to set 'em off as anythin' else. All the time it's like carryin' a light into a fireworks place. Drop it once an' the air 'll be full of sky-rockets, roman candles, pinwheels, an' set pieces till you're that dazed you don't know where you're livin'. Don't never take no red-haired one, my dear, if you're anyways set on peace. I never took but one, but that was enough to set me dead against the breed.

"Well, as I was a-sayin', James begun to woo me in the cemetery. Whenever you see a man in a cemetery, my dear, you can take it for granted that he's a new-made widower. After the first week or two, he ain't got no time to go to no grave, he's so busy lookin' out for the next one. When I see James a-waterin' an' a-weedin' on the next lot to mine, therefore, I knowed his sorrer was new, even though the band of crape on his hat was rusty an' old.

"Bein' fellow-mourners, in a way, we struck up kind of a melancholy friendship, an' finally got to borrerin' water from each other's sprinklin' cans an' exchangin' flower seeds an' slips, an' even hull plants. That old deceiver told me it was his first wife that was a-lyin' there, an' showed me her name on the monumint. She was buried in her own folks' lot, an' I never knowed till it was too late that his own lot was plum full of wives, an' this here was a annex, so to speak. I dunno how I come to be so took in, but anyways, when James's grief had subsided somewhat, we decided to travel on the remanin' stretch through this vale of tears together.

---

111

"He told me he had a beautiful home in Taylorville, but was a-livin' where he was so 's to be near the cemetery an' where he could look after dear Annie's grave. The sentiment made me think all the more of him, so 's I didn't hesitate, an' was even willin' to be married with one of my old rings, to save the expense of a new one. James allers was thrifty, an' the way he put it, it sounded quite reasonable, so 's that's how it comes, my dear, that in spite of havin' had seven husbands, I've only got six weddin'-rings.

"I put each one on when its own proper anniversary comes around an' wear it till the next one, when I change again, though for one of the rings it makes only one day, because the fourth and seventh times I was married so near together. That sounds queer, my dear, but if you think it over, you'll see what I mean. It's fortunate, too, in a way, 'cause I found out by accident years afterward that my fourth weddin'-ring come out of a pawn-shop, an' I never took much joy out of wearin' it. Bein' just alike, I wore another one mostly, even when Samuel was alive, but he never noticed. Besides, I reckon 't wouldn't make no difference, for a man that'll go to a pawn-shop for a weddin'-ring ain't one to make a row about his wife's changin' it. When I spoke sharp to him about it, he snickered, an' said it was appropriate enough, though to this day I've never figured out precisely just what the old serpent meant by it.

"Well, as I was sayin', my dear, the minister married us in good an' proper form, an' I must say that, though I've had all kinds of ceremonies, I take to the 'Piscopal one the most, in spite of havin' been brought up Methodis', an' hereafter I'll be married by it if the occasion should arise—an' we drove over to Taylorville.

"The roads was dretful, but bein' experienced in marriage, I could see that it wasn't that that was makin' James drop the whip, an' pull back on the lines when he wanted the horses to go faster, an' not hear things I was a-sayin' to him. Finally, I says, very distinct: 'James, dear, how many children did you say you had?'

"'Eight,' says he, clearin' his throat proud and haughty like.

"'You're lyin',' says I, 'an' you know you're lyin'. You allers told me you had three.'

"'I was speakin' of those by my first wife,' says he. 'My other wives all left one apiece. Ain't I never told you about 'em? I thought I had,' he went on, speakin' quick, 'but if I haven't, it 's because your beauty has made me forget all the pain an' sorrer of the past.'

"With that he clicked to the horses so sudden that I was near threw out of the rig, but it wasn't half so bad as the other jolt he'd just give me. For a long time I didn't say nothin', an' there's nothin' that makes a man so uneasy as a woman that don't say nothin', my dear, so you just write that down in your little book, an' remember it. It'll come in handy long before you're through with your first marriage an' have begun on your second. Havin' been through four, I was well skilled in keepin' my mouth shut, an' I never said a word till we drove into the yard of the most disconsolate-lookin' premises I ever seen since I was took to the poorhouse on a visit.

"'James,' says I, cool but firm, 'is this your magnificent residence?'

"'It is,' says he, very soft, 'an' it is here that I welcome my bride. Have you ever seen anythin' like this view?'

"'No,' says I, 'I never have'; an' it was gospel truth I was speakin', too, for never before had I been to a place where the pigsty was in front.

"'It is a wonderful view,' says I, sarcastic like, 'but before I linger to admire it more, I would love to look upon the scenery inside the house.'

"When we went in, I thought I was either dreamin' or had got to Bedlam. The seven youngest children was raisin' particular Cain, an' the oldest, a pretty little girl of thirteen, was doin' her best to quiet 'em. There was six others besides what had been accounted for, but I soon found that they belonged to a neighbour, an' was just visitin' to relieve the monotony.

"The woman James had left takin' care of 'em had been gone two weeks an' more, with a month's wages still comin' to her, which James never felt called on to pay, on account of her havin' left without notice. James was dretful thrifty. The youngest one was puttin' the cat into the water-pitcher, an' as soon as I found out what his name was, I called him sharp by it an' told him to quit. He put his tongue out at me as sassy as you please, an' says: 'I won't.'

"Well, my dear, I didn't wait to hear no more, but I opened my satchel an' took out one of my slippers an' give that child a lickin' that he'll remember when he's a grandparent. 'Hereafter,' says I, 'when I tell you to do anythin', you'll do it. I'll speak kind the first time an' firm the second, and the third time the whole thing will be illustrated so plain that nobody can't misunderstand it. Your pa has took me into a confidence game,' says I, speakin' to all the children, 'but I was never one to draw back from what I'd put my hand to, an' I aim to do right by you if you do right by me. You mind,' says I, 'an' you won't have no trouble; an' the same thing,' says I to James, 'applies to you.'

"I felt sorry for all those poor little motherless things, with a liar for a pa, an' all the time I lived there, I tried to make up to 'em what I could, but step-mas have their sorrers, my dear, that's what they do, an' I ain't never seen no piece about it in the paper yet, either.

"If you'll excuse me now, my dear, I'll go to my room. It's just come to my mind now that this here is one of my anniversaries, an' I'll have to look up the facts in my family Bible, an' change my ring."

At dinner-time the chastised and chastened twin appeared in freshly starched raiment. His eyes were swollen and his face flushed, but otherwise his recent painful experience had remarkably improved him. He said "please" and "thank you," and did not even resent it when Willie slyly dropped a small piece of watermelon down his neck.

"This afternoon," said Elaine, "Mr. Perkins composed a beautiful poem. I know it is beautiful, though I have not yet heard it. I do not wish to be selfish in my pleasure, so I will ask him to read it to us all."

The poet's face suddenly became the colour of his hair. He dropped his napkin, and swiftly whispered to Elaine, while he was picking it up, that she herself was the subject of the poem.

"How perfectly charming," said Elaine, clearly. "Did you hear, Mrs. Carr? Poor little, insignificant me has actually inspired a great poem. Oh, do read it, Mr. Perkins? We are all dying to hear it!"

Fairly cornered, the poet muttered that he had lost it—some other time—wait until to-morrow—and so on.

"No need to wait," said Dick, with an ironical smile. "It was lost, but now is found. I came upon it myself, blowing around unheeded under the library window, quite like a common bit of paper."

Mr. Perkins was transfixed with amazement, for his cherished poem was at that minute in his breast pocket. He clutched at it spasmodically, to be sure it was still safe.

Very different emotions possessed Harlan, who choked on his food. He instinctively guessed the worst, and saw his home in lurid ruin about him, but was powerless to avert the catastrophe.

"Read it, Dick," said Mrs. Dodd, kindly. "We are all a-perishin' to hear it. I can't eat another bite until I do. I reckon it'll sound like a valentine," she concluded, with a malicious glance at Mr. Perkins.

"I have taken the liberty," chuckled Dick, "of changing a word or two occasionally, to make better sense of it, and of leaving out some lines altogether. Every one is privileged to vary an established form." Without further preliminary, he read the improved version.


"The little doggie sheds his coat,

Elaine, have you forgotten?

What is it goes around a button?

I thought you knew that simple thing,

But ideas in your head take wing.

Elaine, have you forgotten?

The answer is a goat.

"How much is three times humpty-steen?

Elaine, have you forgotten?

Why does a chicken cross the road?

Who carries home a toper's load?

You are so very stupid, dear!

Elaine, have you forgotten?

"You think a mop of scarlet hair

And pale green eyes——"

"That will do," said Miss St. Clair, crisply. "Mr. Perkins, may I ask as a favour that you will not speak to me again?" She marched out with her head high, and Mr. Perkins, wholly unstrung, buried his face in his napkin.

Harlan laughed—a loud, ringing laugh, such as Dorothy had not heard from him for months, and striding around the table, he grasped Dick's hand in tremendous relief.

"Let me have it," he cried, eagerly. "Give me all of it!"

"Sure," said Dick, readily, passing over both sheets of paper.

Harlan went into the library with the composition, and presently, when Dick was walking around the house and saw bits of torn paper fluttering out of the open window, a light broke through his usual density.

"Whew!" he said to himself. "I'll be darned! I'll be everlastingly darned! Idiot!" he continued, savagely. "Oh, if I could only kick myself! Poor Dorothy! I wonder if she knows!"

# XV

## Treasure-Trove

The August moon swung high in the heavens, and the crickets chirped unbearably. The luminous dew lay heavily upon the surrounding fields, and now and then a stray breeze, amid the overhanging branches of the trees that lined the roadway, aroused in the consciousness of the single wayfarer a feeling closely akin to panic. When he reached the summit of the hill, he was trembling violently.

In the dooryard of the Jack-o'-Lantern, he paused. It was dark, save for a single round window. In an upper front room a night-lamp, turned low, gave one leering eye to the grotesque exterior of the house.

With his heart thumping loudly, Mr. Bradford leaned against a tree and divested himself of his shoes. From a package under his arm, he took out a pair of soft felt slippers, the paper rattling loudly as he did so. He put them on, hesitated, then went cautiously up the walk.

"In all my seventy-eight years," he thought, "I have never done anything like this. If I had not promised the Colonel—but a promise to a dying man is sacred, especially when he is one's best friend."

The sound of the key in the lock seemed almost like an explosion of dynamite. Mr. Bradford wiped the cold perspiration from his forehead, turned the door slowly upon its squeaky hinges, and went in, feeling like a burglar.

"I am not a burglar," he thought, his hands shaking. "I have come to give, not to take away."

Fearfully, he tiptoed into the parlour, expecting at any moment to arouse the house. Feeling his way carefully along the wall, and guided by the moonlight which streamed in at the side windows, he came to the wing occupied by Mrs. Holmes and her exuberant offspring. Here he stooped, awkwardly, and slipped a sealed and addressed letter under the door, heaving a sigh of relief as he got away without having wakened any one.

The sounds which came from Mrs. Dodd's room were reassuringly suggestive of sleep. Hastily, he slipped another letter under her door, then made his way cautiously to the kitchen. The missive intended for Mrs. Smithers was left on the door-mat outside, for, as Mr. Bradford well knew, the ears of the handmaiden were uncomfortably keen.

At the foot of the stairs he hesitated again, but by the time he reached the top, his heart had ceased to beat audibly. He tiptoed down the corridor to Uncle Israel's room, then, further on, to Dick's. The letter intended for Mr. Perkins was slipped under Elaine's door, Mr. Bradford not being aware that the poet had changed his room. Having safely accomplished his last errand, the tension relaxed, and he went downstairs with more assurance, his pace being unduly hastened by a subdued howl from one of the twins.

Bidding himself be calm, he got to the front door, and drew a long breath of relief as he closed it noiselessly. There was a light in Mrs. Holmes's room now, and Mr. Bradford did not wish to linger. He gathered up his shoes and fairly ran downhill, arriving at his office much shaken in mind and body, nearly two hours after he had started.

"I do not know," he said to himself, "why the Colonel should have been so particular as to dates and hours, but he knew his own business best." Then, further in accordance with his instructions, he burned a number of letters which could not be delivered personally.

If Mr. Bradford could have seen the company which met at the breakfast table the following morning, he would have been amply repaid for his supreme effort of the night before, had he been blessed with any sense of humour at all. The Carrs were untroubled, and Elaine appeared as usual, except for her haughty indifference to Mr. Perkins. She thought he had written a letter to himself and slipped it under her door, in order to compel her to speak to him, but she had tactfully avoided that difficulty by leaving it on his own threshold. Dick's eyes were dancing and at intervals his mirth bubbled over, needlessly, as every one else appeared to think.

"I doesn't know wot folks finds to laugh at," remarked Mrs. Smithers, as she brought in the coffee; "that's wot I doesn't. It's a solemn time, I take it, when the sheeted spectres of the dead walks abroad by night, that's wot it is. It's time for folks to be thinkin' about their immortal souls."

This enigmatical utterance produced a startling effect. Mr. Perkins turned a pale green and hastily excused himself, his breakfast wholly untouched. Mrs. Holmes dropped her fork and recovered it in evident confusion. Mrs. Dodd's face was a bright scarlet and appeared about to burst, but she kept her lips compressed into a thin, tight line. Uncle Israel nodded over his predigested food. "Just so," he mumbled; "a solemn time."

Eagerly watching for an opportunity, Mrs. Holmes dived into the barn, and emerged, cautiously, with the spade concealed under her skirts. She carried it into her own apartment and hid it under Willie's bed. Mrs. Smithers went to look for it a little later, and, discovering that it was unaccountably missing, excavated her own private spade from beneath the hay. During the afternoon, the poet was observed lashing the fire-shovel to the other end of a decrepit rake. Uncle Israel, after a fruitless search of the premises, actually went to town and came back with a bulky and awkward parcel, which he hid in the shrubbery.

Meanwhile, Willie had gone whimpering to Mrs. Dodd, who was in serious trouble of her own. "I'm afraid," he admitted, when closely questioned.

"Afraid of what?" demanded his counsellor, sharply.

"I'm afraid of ma," sobbed Willie. "She's a-goin' to bury me. She's got the spade hid under my bed now."

Sudden emotion completely changed Mrs. Dodd's countenance. "There, there, Willie," she said, stroking him kindly. "Where is your ma?"

"She's out in the orchard with Ebbie and Rebbie."

"Well now, deary, don't you say nothin' at all to your ma, an' we'll fool her. The idea of buryin' a nice little boy like you! You just go an' get me that spade an' I'll hide it in my room. Then, when your ma asks for it, you don't know nothin' about it. See?"

Willie's troubled face brightened, and presently the implement was under Mrs. Dodd's own bed, and her door locked. Much relieved in his mind and cherishing kindly sentiments toward his benefactor, Willie slid down the banisters, unrebuked, the rest of the afternoon.

Meanwhile Mrs. Dodd sat on the porch and meditated. "I'd never have thought," she said to herself, "that Ebeneezer would intend that Holmes woman to have any of it, but you never can tell what folks'll do when their minds gets to failin' at the end. Ebeneezer's mind must have failed dretful, for I know he didn't make no promise to her, same as he did to me, an' if she don't suspect nothin', what did she go an' get the spade for? Dretful likely hand it is, for spirit writin'."

Looking about furtively to make sure that she was not observed, Mrs. Dodd drew out of the mysterious recesses of her garments, the crumpled communication of the night before. It was dated, "Heaven, August 12th," and the penmanship was Uncle Ebeneezer's to the life.

"Dear Belinda," it read. "I find myself at the last moment obliged to change my plans. If you will go to the orchard at exactly twelve o'clock on the night of August 1th, you will find there what you seek. Go straight ahead to the ninth row of apple trees, then seven trees to the left. A cat's skull hangs from the lower branch, if it hasn't blown down or been taken away. Dig here and you will find a tin box containing what I have always meant you to have.

"I charge you by all you hold sacred to obey these directions in every particular, and unless you want to lose it all, to say nothing about it to any one who may be in the house.

"I am sorry to put you to this inconvenience, but the limitations of the spirit world cannot well be explained to mortals. I hope you will make a wise use of the money and not spend it all on clothes, as women are apt to do.

"In conclusion, let me say that I am very happy in heaven, though it is considerably more quiet than any place I ever lived in before. I have met a great many friends here, but no relatives except my wife. Farewell, as I shall probably never see you again.

"Yours,

"Ebeneezer Judson.

"P.S. All of your previous husbands are here, in the sunny section set aside for martyrs. None of them give you a good reputation.

"E. J."

"Don't it beat all," muttered Mrs. Dodd to herself, excitedly. "Here was Ebeneezer at my door last night, an' I never knowed it. Sakes alive, if I had knowed it, I wouldn't have slep' like I did. Here comes that Holmes hussy. Wonder what she knows!"

"Do you believe in spirits, Mrs. Dodd?" inquired Mrs. Holmes, in a careless tone that did not deceive her listener.

"Depends," returned the other, with an evident distaste for the subject.

"Do you believe spirits can walk?"

"I ain't never seen no spirits walk, but I've seen folks try to walk that was full of spirits, and there wa'n't no visible improvement in their steppin'." This was a pleasant allusion to the departed Mr. Holmes, who was currently said to have "drunk hisself to death."

A scarlet flush, which mounted to the roots of Mrs. Holmes's hair, indicated that the shot had told, and Mrs. Dodd went to her own room, where she carefully locked herself in. She was determined to sit upon her precious spade until midnight, if it were necessary, to keep it.

Mrs. Smithers was sitting up in bed with the cold perspiration oozing from every pore, when the kitchen clock struck twelve sharp, quick strokes. The other clocks in the house took up the echo and made merry with it. The grandfather's clock in the hall was the last to strike, and the twelve deep-toned notes boomed a solemn warning which, to more than one quaking listener, bore a strong suggestion of another world—an uncanny world at that.

"Guess I'll go along," said Dick to himself, yawning and stretching. "I might just as well see the fun."

Mrs. Smithers, with her private spade and her odorous lantern, was at the spot first, closely seconded by Mrs. Dodd, in a voluminous garment of red flannel which had seen all of its best days and not a few of its worst. Trembling from head to foot, came Mrs. Holmes, carrying a pair of shears, which she had snatched up at the last moment when she discovered the spade was missing. Mr. Perkins, fully garbed, appeared with his improvised shovel. Uncle Israel, in his piebald dressing-gown, tottered along in the rear, bearing his spade, still unwrapped, his bedroom candle, and a box of matches. Dick surveyed the scene from a safe, shadowy distance, and on a branch near the skull, Claudius Tiberius was stretched at full length, purring with a loud, resonant purr which could be heard from afar.

After the first shock of surprise, which was especially keen on the part of Mrs. Dodd, when she saw Uncle Israel in the company, Mrs. Smithers broke the silence.

"It's nothink more nor a wild-goose chase," she said, resentfully. "A-gettin' us all out'n our beds at this time o' night! It's a sufferin' and dyin' shame, that's wot it is, and if sperrits was like other folks, 't wouldn't 'ave happened."

"Sarah," said Mrs. Dodd, firmly, "keep your mouth shut. Israel, will you dig?"

"We'll all dig," said Mrs. Holmes, in the voice of authority, and thereafter the dirt flew briskly enough, accompanied by the laboured breathing of perspiring humanity.

It was Uncle Israel's spade that first touched the box, and, with a cry of delight, he stooped for it, as did everybody else. By sheer force of muscle, Mrs. Dodd got it away from him.

"This wrangle," sighed Mr. Perkins, "is both unseemly and sordid. Let us all agree to abide by dear Uncle Ebeneezer's last bequests."

"There won't be no desire not to abide by 'em," snorted Mrs. Smithers, "wot with cats as can't stay buried and sheeted spectres of the dead a-walkin' through the house by night!"

By this time, Mrs. Dodd had the box open, and a cry of astonishment broke from her lips. Several heads were badly bumped in the effort to peep into the box, and an unprotected sneeze from Uncle Israel added to the general unpleasantness.

"You can all go away," cried Mrs. Dodd, shrilly. "There's two one-dollar bills here, two quarters, an' two nickels an' eight pennies. 'T aint nothin' to be fit over."

"But the letter," suggested Mr. Perkins, hopefully. "Is there not a letter from dear Uncle Ebeneezer? Let us gather around the box in a reverent spirit and listen to dear Uncle Ebeneezer's last words."

"You can read 'em," snapped Mrs. Holmes, "if you're set on hearing."

Uncle Israel wheezed so loudly that for the moment he drowned the deep purr of Claudius Tiberius. When quiet was restored, Mr. Perkins broke the seal of the envelope and unfolded the communication within. Uncle Israel held the dripping candle on one side and Mrs. Smithers the smoking lantern on the other, while near by, Dick watched the midnight assembly with an unholy glee which, in spite of his efforts, nearly became audible.

"How beautiful," said Mr. Perkins, "to think that dear Uncle Ebeneezer's last words should be given to us in this unexpected but original way."

"Shut up," said Mrs. Smithers, emphatically, "and read them last words. I'm gettin' the pneumony now, that's wot I am."

"You're the only one," chirped Mrs. Dodd, hysterically. "The money in this here box is all old." It was, indeed. Mr. Judson seemed to have purposely chosen ragged bills and coins worn smooth.

"'Dear Relations,'" began Mr. Perkins. "'As every one of you have at one time or another routed me out of bed to let you in when you have come to my house on the night train, and always uninvited——'"

"I never did," interrupted Mrs. Holmes. "I always came in the daytime."

"Nobody ain't come at night," explained Mrs. Smithers, "since 'e fixed the 'ouse over into a face. One female fainted dead away when 'er started up the hill and see it a-winkin' at 'er, yes sir, that's wot 'er did!"

"'It seems only fitting and appropriate,'" continued Mr. Perkins, "'that you should all see how it seems.'" The poet wiped his massive brow with his soiled handkerchief. "Dear uncle!" he commented.

"Yes," wheezed Uncle Israel, "'dear uncle!' Damn his stingy old soul," he added, with uncalled-for emphasis.

"It gives me pleasure to explain in this fashion my disposal of my estate," the reader went on, huskily.

"Of all the connection on both sides, there is only one that has never been to see me, unless I've forgotten some, and that is my beloved nephew, James Harlan Carr."

"Him," creaked Uncle Israel. "Him, as never see Ebeneezer."

"He has never," continued the poet, with difficulty, "rung my door bell at night, nor eaten me out of house and home, nor written begging letters—" this phrase was well-nigh inaudible—"nor had fits on me——"

Here there was a pause and all eyes were fastened upon Uncle Israel.

"'T wa'n't a fit!" he screamed. "It was a involuntary spasm brought on by takin' two searchin' medicines too near together. 'T wa'n't a fit!"

"Nor children——"

"The idea!" snapped Mrs. Holmes. "Poor little Ebbie and Rebbie had to be born somewhere."

"Nor paralysis——"

"That was Cousin Si Martin," said Mrs. Dodd, half to herself. "He was took bad with it in the night."

"He has never come to spend Christmas with me and remained until the ensuing dog days, nor sent me a crayon portrait of himself"—Mr. Perkins faltered here, but nobly went on—"nor had typhoid fever, nor finished up his tuberculosis, nor cut teeth, nor set the house on fire with a bath cabinet——"

At this juncture Uncle Israel was so overcome with violent emotion that it was some time before the reading could proceed.

"Never having come into any kind of relations with my dear nephew, James Harlan Carr," continued Mr. Perkins, in troubled tones, "I have shown my gratitude in this humble way. To him I give the house and all my furniture, my books and personal effects of every kind, my farm in Hill County, two thousand acres, all improved and clear of incumbrance, except blooded stock,——"

"I never knowed 'e 'ad no farm," interrupted Mrs. Smithers.

"And the ten thousand and eighty-four dollars in the City Bank which at this writing is there to my credit, but will be duly transferred, and my dear Rebecca's diamond pin to be given to my beloved nephew's wife when he marries. It is all in my will, which my dear friend Jeremiah Bradford has, and which he will read at the proper time to those concerned."

"The old snake!" shrieked Mrs. Holmes.

"Further," went on the poet, almost past speech by this time, "I direct that the remainder of my estate, which is here in this box, shall be divided as follows:

"Eight cents each to that loafer, Si Martin, his lazy wife, and their eight badly brought-up children, with instructions to be generous to any additions to said children through matrimony or natural causes; Fanny Wood and that poor, white-livered creature she married, thereby proving her own idiocy if it needed proof; Uncle James's cross-eyed third wife and her two silly daughters; Rebecca's sister's scoundrelly second husband, with his foolish wife and their little boy with a face like a pug dog; Uncle Jason, who has needed a bath ever since I knew him—I want he should spend his legacy for soap—and his epileptic stepson, whose name I forget, though he lived with me five years hand-running; lying Sally Simmons and her half-witted daughter; that old hen, Belinda Dodd; that skunk, Harold Vernon Perkins, who never did a stroke of honest work in his life till he began to dig for this box; monkey-faced Lucretia and the four thieving little Riley children, who are likely to get into prison when they grow up; that human undertaker's waggon, Betsey Skiles, and her two impudent nieces; that grand old perambulating drug store, Israel Skiles; that Holmes fool with the three reprints of her ugliness—eight cents apiece, and may you get all possible good out of it.

"Dick Chester, however, having always paid his board, and tried to be a help to me in several small ways, and in spite of having lived with me eight Summers or more without having been asked to do so, gets two thousand two hundred and fifty dollars which is deposited for him in the savings department of the Metropolitan Bank, plus the three hundred and seventy dollars he paid me for board without my asking him for it. Sarah Smithers, being in the main a good woman, though sharp-tongued at times, and having been faithful all the time my house has been full of lowdown cusses too lazy to work for their living, gets twelve hundred and fifty dollars which is in the same bank as Dick's. The rest of you take your eight cents apiece and be damned. You can get the money changed at the store. If any have been left out, it is my desire that those remembered should divide with the unfortunate.

"If you had not all claimed to be Rebecca's relatives, you would have been kicked out of my house years ago, but since writing this, I have seen Rebecca and made it right with her. It was not her desire that I should be imposed upon.

"Get out of my house, every one of you, before noon to-morrow, and the devil has my sincere sympathy when you go to live with him and make hell what you have made my house ever since Rebecca's death. Get out!!!

"Ebeneezer Judson."

The letter was badly written and incoherent, yet there could be no doubt of its meaning, nor of the state of mind in which it had been penned. For a moment, there was a tense silence, then Mrs. Dodd tittered hysterically.

"We thought diamonds was goin' to be trumps," she observed, "an' it turned out to be spades."

Uncle Israel wheezed again and Mrs. Smithers smacked her lips with intense satisfaction. Mrs. Holmes was pale with anger, and, under cover of the night, Dick sneaked back to his room, shame-faced, yet happy. Claudius Tiberius still purred, sticking his claws into the bark with every evidence of pleasure.

"I do not know," said Mr. Perkins, sadly, running his fingers through his mane, "whether we are obliged to take as final these vagaries of a dying man. Dear Uncle Ebeneezer could not have been sane when he penned this cruel letter. I do not believe it was his desire to have any of us go away before the usual time." Under cover of these forgiving sentiments, he pocketed all the money in the box.

"Me neither," said Mrs. Dodd. "Anyhow, I'm goin' to stay. No sheeted spectre can't scare me away from a place I've always stayed in Summers, 'specially," she added, sarcastically, "when I'm remembered in the will."

Mrs. Smithers clucked disagreeably and went back to the house. Uncle Israel looked after her with dismay. "Do you suppose," he queried, in falsetto, "that she'll tell the Carrs?"

"Hush, Israel," replied Mrs. Dodd. "She can't tell them Carrs about our diggin' all night in the orchard, 'cause she was here herself. They didn't get no spirit communication an' they won't suspect nothin'. We'll just stay where we be an' go on 's if nothin' had happened."

Indeed, this seemed the wisest plan, and, shivering with the cold, the baffled ones filed back to the Jack-o'-Lantern. "How did you get out, Israel?" whispered Mrs. Dodd, as they approached the house.

The old man snickered. It was the only moment of the evening he had thoroughly enjoyed. "The same spirit that give me the letter, Belinda," he returned, pleasantly, "also give me a key. You didn't think I had no flyin' machine, did you?"

"Humph" grunted Mrs. Dodd. "Spirits don't carry no keys!"

At the threshold they paused, the sensitive poet quite unstrung by the night's adventure. From the depths of the Jack-o'-Lantern came a shrill, infantile cry.

"Is that Ebbie," asked Mrs. Dodd, "or Rebbie?"

Mrs. Holmes turned upon her with suppressed fury. "Don't you ever dare to allude to my children in that manner again," she commanded, hoarsely.

"What is their names?" quavered Uncle Israel, lighting his candle.

"Their names," returned Mrs. Holmes, with a vast accession of dignity, "are Gladys Gwendolen and Algernon Paul! Good night!"

Just before dawn, a sheeted spectre appeared at the side of Sarah Smither's bed, and swore the trembling woman to secrecy. It was long past sunrise before the frightened handmaiden came to her senses enough to recall that the voice of the apparition had been strangely like Mrs. Dodd's.

# XVI

## Good Fortune

The next morning, Harlan and Dorothy ate breakfast by themselves. There was suppressed excitement in the manner of Mrs. Smithers, who by this time had quite recovered from her fright, and, as they readily saw, not wholly of an unpleasant kind. From time to time she tittered audibly—a thing which had never happened before.

"It's just as if a tombstone should giggle," remarked Harlan. His tone was low, but unfortunately, it carried well.

"Tombstone or not, just as you like," responded Mrs. Smithers, as she came in with the bacon. "I'd be careful 'ow I spoke disrespectfully of tombstones if I was in your places, that's wot I would. Tombstones is kind to some and cussed to others, that's wot they are, and if you don't like the monument wot's at present in your kitchen, you know wot you can do."

After breakfast, she beckoned Dorothy into the kitchen, and "gave notice."

"Oh, Mrs. Smithers," cried Dorothy, almost moved to tears, "please don't leave me in the lurch! What should I do without you, with all these people on my hands? Don't think of such a thing as leaving me!"

"Miss Carr," said Mrs. Smithers, solemnly, with one long bony finger laid alongside of her hooked nose, "'t ain't necessary for you to run no Summer hotel, that's what it ain't. These 'ere all be relations of your uncle's wife and none of his'n except by marriage. Wot's more, your uncle don't want 'em 'ere, that's wot 'e don't."

Mrs. Smithers's tone was so confident that for the moment Dorothy was startled, remembering yesterday's vague allusion to "sheeted spectres of the dead."

"What do you mean?" she demanded.

"Miss Carr," returned Mrs. Smithers, with due dignity, "ever since I come 'ere, I've been invited to shut my 'ead whenever I opened it about that there cat or your uncle or anythink, as you well knows. I was never one wot was fond of 'avin' my 'ead shut up."

"Go on," said Dorothy, her curiosity fully alive, "and tell me what you mean."

"You gives me your solemn oath, Miss, that you won't tell me to shut my 'ead?" queried Mrs. Smithers.

"Of course," returned Dorothy, trying to be practical, though the atmosphere was sepulchral enough.

"Well, then, you knows wot I told you about that there cat. 'E was kilt by your uncle, that's wot 'e was, and your uncle couldn't never abide cats. 'E was that feared of 'em 'e couldn't even bury 'em when they was kilt, and one of my duties, Miss, as long as I lived with 'im, was buryin' of cats, and until this one, I never come up with one wot couldn't stay buried, that's wot I 'aven't.

"'E 'ated 'em like poison, that's wot 'e did. The week afore your uncle died, he kilt this 'ere cat wot's chasin' the chickens now, and I buried 'im with my own hands, but could 'e stay buried? 'E could not. No sooner is your uncle dead and gone than this 'ere cat comes back, and it's the truth, Miss Carr, for where 'e was buried, there ain't no sign of a cat now. Wot's worse, this 'ere cat looks per-cisely like your uncle, green eyes, white shirt front, black tie and all. It's enough to give a body the shivers to see 'im a-settin' on the kitchen floor lappin' up 'is mush and milk, the which your uncle was so powerful fond of.

"Wot's more," continued Mrs. Smithers, in tones of awe, "I'll a'most bet my immortal soul that if you'll dig in the cemetery where your uncle was buried good and proper, you won't find nothin' but the empty coffin and maybe 'is grave clothes. Your uncle's been livin' with us all along in that there cat," she added, triumphantly. "It's 'is punishment, for 'e couldn't never abide 'em, that's wot 'e couldn't."

Mrs. Carr opened her mouth to speak, then, remembering her promise, took refuge in flight.

"'Er's scared," muttered Mrs. Smithers, "and no wonder. Wot with cats as can't stay buried, writin' letters and deliverin' 'em in the dead of night, and a purrin' like mad while blamed fools digs for eight cents, most folks would be scared, I take it, that's wot they would."

Dorothy was pale when she went into the library where Harlan was at work. He frowned at the interruption and Dorothy smiled back at him—it seemed so normal and sane.

"What is it, Dorothy?" he asked, not unkindly.

"Oh—just Mrs. Smithers's nonsense. She's upset me."

"What about, dear?" Harlan put his work aside readily enough now.

"Oh, the same old story about the cat and Uncle Ebeneezer. And I'm afraid——"

"Afraid of what?"

"I know it's foolish, but I'm afraid she's going to dig in the cemetery to see if Uncle Ebeneezer is still there. She thinks he's in the cat."

For the moment, Harlan thought Dorothy had suddenly lost her reason, then he laughed heartily.

"Don't worry," he said, "she won't do anything of the kind, and, besides, what if she did? It's a free country, isn't it?"

"And—there's another thing, Harlan." For days she had dreaded to speak of it, but now it could be put off no longer.

"It's—it's money," she went on, unwillingly. "I'm afraid I haven't managed very well, or else it's cost so much for everything, but we're—we're almost broke, Harlan," she concluded, bravely, trying to smile.

Harlan put his hands in his pockets and began to walk back and forth. "If I can only finish the book," he said, at length, "I think we'll be all right, but I can't leave it now. There's only two more chapters to write, and then——"

"And then," cried Dorothy, her beautiful belief in him transfiguring her face, "then we'll be rich, won't we?"

"I am already rich," returned Harlan, "when you have such faith in me as that."

For a moment the shimmering veil of estrangement which so long had hung between them, seemed to part, and reveal soul to soul. As swiftly the mood changed and Dorothy felt it first, like a chill mist in the air. Neither dreamed that with the writing of the first paragraph in the book, the spell had claimed one of them for ever—that cobweb after cobweb, of gossamer fineness, should make a fabric never to be broken; that on one side of it should stand a man who had exchanged his dreams for realities and his realities for dreams, and on the other, a woman, blindly hurt, eternally straining to see beyond the veil.

"What can we do?" asked Harlan, unwontedly practical for the nonce.

"I don't know," said Dorothy. "There are the diamonds, you know, that we found. I don't care for any diamonds, except the one you gave me. If we could sell those——"

"Dorothy, don't. I don't believe they're ours, and if they were, they shouldn't be sold. You should keep them."

"My engagement ring, then," suggested Dorothy, her lips trembling. "That's ours."

"Don't be foolish," said Harlan, a little roughly. "I'll finish this and then we'll see what's to be done."

Feeling her dismissal, Dorothy went out, and, all unknowingly, straight into the sunshine.

Elaine was coming downstairs, fresh and sweet as the morning itself. "Am I too late to have any breakfast, Mrs. Carr?" she asked, gaily. "I know I don't deserve any."

"Of course you shall have breakfast. I'll see to it."

Elaine took her place at the table and Dorothy, reluctant to put further strain on the frail bond that anchored Mrs. Smithers to her service, brought in the breakfast herself. "You're so good to me," said the girl, gratefully, as Dorothy poured out a cup of steaming coffee. "To think how beautiful you've been to me, when I never saw either one of you in my whole life, till I came here ill and broken-hearted! See what you've made of me—see how well and strong I am!"

Swiftly, Dorothy bent and kissed Elaine, a strange, shadowy cloud for ever lifted from her heart. She had not known how heavy it was nor how charged with foreboding, until it was gone.

"I want to do something for you," Elaine went on, laughing to hide the mist in her eyes, "and I've just thought what I can do. My mother had some beautiful old mahogany furniture, just loads of it, and some wonderful laces, and I'm going to divide with you."

"No, you're not," returned Dorothy, warmly. She felt that Elaine had already given her enough.

"It isn't meant for payment, Mrs. Carr," the girl went on, her big blue eyes fixed upon Dorothy, "but you're to take it from me just as I've taken this lovely Summer from you. You took in a stranger, weak and helpless and half-crazed with grief, and you've made her into a happy woman again."

Before Dorothy could answer, Dick lounged in, frankly sleepy. "Second call in the dining car?" he asked, taking Mrs. Dodd's place, across the table from Elaine.

"Third call," returned Dorothy, brightly, "and, if you don't mind, I'll leave you two to wait on yourselves." She went upstairs, her heart light, not so much from reality as from prescience. "How true it is," she thought, "that if you only wait and do the best you can, things all work out straight again. I've had to learn it, but I know it now."

"Bully bunch, the Carrs," remarked Dick, pushing his cup to Elaine.

"They're lovely," she answered, with conviction.

The sun streamed brightly into the dining-room of the Jack-o'-Lantern and changed its hideousness into cheer. Seeing Elaine across from him, gracefully pouring his coffee, affected Dick strangely. Since the day before, he had seen clearly something which he must do.

"I say, Elaine," he began, awkwardly. "That beast of a poem I read the other day——"

Her face paled, ever so slightly. "Yes?"

"Well, Perkins didn't write it, you know," Dick went on, hastily. "I did it myself. Or, rather I found it, blowing around, outside, just as I said, and I fixed it."

At length he became restless under the calm scrutiny of Elaine's clear eyes. "I beg your pardon," he continued.

"Did you think," she asked, "that it was nice to make fun of a lady in that way?"

"I didn't think," returned Dick, truthfully. "I never thought for a minute that it was making fun of you, but only of that—that pup, Perkins," he concluded, viciously.

"Under the circumstances," said Elaine, ignoring the epithet, "the silence of Mr. Perkins has been very noble. I shall tell him so."

"Do," answered Dick, with difficulty. "He's ambling up to the lunch-counter now." Mr. Chester went out by way of the window, swallowing hard.

"I have just been told," said Miss St. Clair to the poet, "that the—er—poem was not written by you, and I apologise for what I said."

Mr. Perkins bowed in acknowledgment. "It is a small matter," he said, wearily, running his fingers through his hair. It was, indeed, compared with deep sorrow of a penetrating kind, and a sleepless night, but Elaine did not relish the comment.

"Were—were you restless in the night?" she asked, conventionally.

"I was. I did not sleep at all until after four o'clock, and then only for a few moments."

"I'm sorry. Did—did you write anything?"

"I began an epic," answered the poet, touched, for the moment, by this unexpected sympathy. "An epic in blank verse, on 'Disappointment.'"

"I'm sure it's beautiful," continued Elaine, coldly. "And that reminds me. I have hunted through my room, in every possible place, and found nothing."

A flood of painful emotion overwhelmed the poet, and he buried his face in his hands. In a flash, Elaine was violently angry, though she could not have told why. She marched out of the dining-room and slammed the door. "Delicate, sensitive soul," she said to herself, scornfully. "Wants people to hunt for money he thinks may be hidden in his room, and yet is so far above sordidness that he can't hear it spoken of!"

Seeing Mr. Chester pacing back and forth moodily at some distance from the house, Elaine rushed out to him. "Dick," she cried, "he *is* a lobster!"

Dick's clouded face brightened. "Is he?" he asked, eagerly, knowing instinctively whom she meant. "Elaine, you're a brick!" They shook hands in token of absolute agreement upon one subject at least, and the girl's right hand hurt her for some little time afterward.

Left to himself, Mr. Perkins mused upon the dread prospect before him. For years he had calculated upon a generous proportion of his Uncle Ebeneezer's estate, and had even borrowed money upon the strength of his expectations. These debts now loomed up inconveniently.

The vulgar, commercial people from whom Mr. Perkins had borrowed filthy coin were quite capable of speaking of the matter, and in an unpleasant manner at that. The fine soul of Mr. Perkins shrank from the ordeal. He had that particular disdain of commercialism which is inseparable from the incapable and unsuccessful, and yet, if the light of his genius were to illuminate a desolate world, Mr. Perkins must have money.

He might even have to degrade himself by coarse toil—and hitherto, he had been too proud to work. The thought was terrible. Pegasus hitched to the plough was nothing compared with the prospect of Mr. Perkins being obliged to earn three or four dollars a week in some humble, common capacity.

Then a bright idea came to his rescue. "Mr. Carr," he thought, "the gentleman who is now entertaining me—he is doing my own kind of work, though of course it is less fine in quality. Perhaps he would like the opportunity of going down to posterity as the humble Mæcenas of a new Horace."

Borne to the library in the rush of this attractive idea, Mr. Perkins opened the door, which Harlan had forgotten to lock, and without in any way announcing himself, broke in on Harlan's chapter.

"What do you mean?" demanded the irate author. "What business have you butting in here like this? Get out!"

"I—" stammered Mr. Perkins.

"Get out!" thundered Harlan. It sounded strangely like the last phrase of "dear Uncle Ebeneezer's last communication," and, trembling, the disconsolate poet obeyed. He fled to his own room as a storm-tossed ship to its last harbour, and renewed the composition of his epic on "Disappointment," for which, by this time, he had additional material.

Harlan went back to his work, but the mood was gone. The living, radiant picture had wholly vanished, and in its place was a heap of dead, dry, meaningless words. "Did I write it?" asked Harlan, of himself, "and if so, why?"

Like the mocking fantasy of a dream as seen in the instant of waking, Elaine and her company had gone, as if to return no more. Only two chapters were yet to be written, and he knew, vaguely, what Elaine was about to do when he left her, but his pen had lost the trick of writing.

Deeply troubled, Harlan went to the window, where the outer world still had the curious appearance of unreality. It was as though a sheet of glass were between him and the life of the rest of the world. He could see through it clearly, but the barrier was there, and must always be there. Upon the edge of this glass, the light of life should break and resolve itself into prismatic colours, of which he should see one at a time, now and then more, and often a clear, pitiless view of the world should give him no colour at all.

Presently Lawyer Bradford came up the hill, dressed for a formal call. In a flash it brought back to Harlan the day the old man had first come to the Jack-o'-Lantern, when Dorothy was a happy girl with a care-free boy for a husband. How much had happened since, and how old and grey the world had grown!

"I desire to see the distinguished author, Mr. Carr," the thin, piping voice was saying at the door, "upon a matter of immediate and personal importance. And Mrs. Carr also, if she is at leisure. Privacy is absolutely essential."

"Come into the library," said Harlan, from the doorway. Another interruption made no difference now. Dorothy soon followed, much mystified by the way in which Mrs. Smithers had summoned her.

Remembering the inopportune intrusion of Mr. Perkins, Harlan locked the door. "Now, Mr. Bradford," he said, easily, "what is it?"

"I should have told you before," began the old lawyer, "had not the bonds of silence been laid upon me by one whom we all revere and who is now past carrying out his own desires. The house is yours, as my letters of an earlier date apprised you, and the will is to be probated at the Fall term of court.

"Your uncle," went on Mr. Bradford, unwillingly, "was a great sufferer from—from relations," he added, lowering his voice to a shrill whisper, "and he has chosen to revenge himself for his sufferings in his own way. Of this I am not at liberty to speak, though no definite silence was required of me later than yesterday.

"There is, however, a farm of two thousand acres, all improved, which is still to come to you, and a sum of money amounting to something over ten thousand dollars, in the bank to your credit. The multitudinous duties in connection with the practice of my profession have prevented me from making myself familiar with the exact amount.

"And," he went on, looking at Dorothy, "there is a very beautiful diamond pin, the gift of my lamented friend to his lovely young wife upon the day of the solemnisation of their nuptials, which was to be given to the wife of Mr. Judson's nephew when he should marry. It is sewn in a mattress in the room at the end of the north wing."

The earth whirled beneath Dorothy's feet. At first, she had not fully comprehended what Mr. Bradford was saying, but now she realised that they had passed from pinching poverty to affluence—at least it seemed so to her. Harlan was not so readily confused, but none the less, he, too, was dazed. Neither of them could speak.

"I should be grateful," the old man was saying, "if you would ask Mr. Richard Chester and Mrs. Sarah Smithers to come to my office at their earliest convenience. I will not trespass upon their valuable time at present."

There was a long silence, during which Mr. Bradford cleared his throat, and wiped his glasses several times. "The farm has always been held in my name," he continued, "to protect our lamented friend and benefactor from additional disturbance. If—if the relations had known, his life would have been even less peaceful than it was. A further farm, valued at twelve thousand dollars, and also held in my name, is my friend's last gift to me, as I discovered by opening a personal letter which was to be kept sealed until this morning. I did not open it until late in the morning, not wishing to show unseemly eagerness to pry into my friend's affairs. I am too much affected to speak of it—I feel his loss too keenly. He was my Colonel—I served under him in the war."

A mist filled the old man's eyes and he fumbled for the door-knob. Harlan found it for him, turned the key, and opened the door. Mrs. Dodd, Mrs. Holmes, Mrs. Smithers, and the suffering poet were all in the hall, their attitudes plainly indicating that they had been listening at the door, but something in Mr. Bradford's face made them huddle back into the corner, ashamed.

Feeling his way with his cane, he went to the parlour door, where he stood for a moment at the threshold, his streaming eyes fixed upon the portrait over the mantel. The simple dignity of his grief forbade a word from any one. At length he straightened himself, brought his trembling hand to his forehead in a feeble military salute, and, wiping his eyes, tottered off downhill.

# XVII

## The Lady Elaine knows her Heart

*It was on a dark and stormy midnight, when the thunders boomed and the dread fury of the lightnings scarred the overhanging cliffs, that the Lady Elaine at last came to know her heart.*

*She was in a cave, safe from all but the noise of the storm. A cheery fire blazed at her door, and her bed within was made soft with pine boughs and skins. For weeks they had journeyed here and there, yet there had been no knight in whose face Elaine could find what she sought.*

*As she lay on her couch, she reflected upon the faithful wayfarers who had travelled with her, who had ever been gentle and courtly, saving her from all annoyance and all harm. Yet above them all, there was one who, from the time of their starting, had kept vigilant guard. He was the humblest of them all, but it was he who made her rest in shady places by the wayside when she herself scarce knew that she was weary; had given her cool spring water in a cup cunningly woven of leaves before she had realised her thirst; had brought her berries and strange, luscious fruits before she had thought of hunger; and who had cheered her, many a time, when no one else had guessed that she was sad.*

*Outside, he was guarding her now, all heedless of the rain. She could see him dimly in the shadow, then, all at once, more clearly in the firelight. His head was bowed and his arms folded, yet in the strong lines of his body there was no hint of weariness. Well did the Lady Elaine know that until Dawn spun her web of enchantment upon the mysterious loom of the East, he would march sleeplessly before her door, replenishing the fire, listening now and then for her deep breathing, and, upon the morrow, gaily tell her of his dreams.*

*Dreams they were, indeed, but not the dreams of sleep. Upon these midnight marchings, her sentinel gave his wandering fancy free rein. And because of the dumb pain in his heart, these fancies were all the merrier; more golden with the sun of laughter, more gemmed with the pearl of tears.*

*Proud-hearted, yet strangely homesick, the Lady Elaine was restless this night. "I must go back," she thought, "to the Castle of Content, where my dear father would fain have his child again. And yet I dread to go back with my errand undone, my quest unrewarded.*

"What is it," thought Elaine, in sudden self-searching, "that I seek? What must this man be, to whom I would surrender the keeping of my heart? What do I ask that is so hard to find?

"Am I seeking for a god? Nay, surely not, but only for a man. Valorous he must be, indeed, but not in the lists—'tis not a soldier, for I have seen them by the hundred since I left my home in the valley. 'Tis not a model for the tapestry weaver that my heart would have, for I have seen the most beautiful youths of my country since I came forth upon my quest.

"Some one, perchance," mused the Lady Elaine, "whose beauty my eyes alone should perceive, whose valour only I should guess before there was need to test it. Some one great of heart and clean of mind, in whose eyes there should never be that which makes a woman ashamed. Some one fine-fibred and strong-souled, not above tenderness when a maid was tired. One who should make a shield of his love, to keep her not only from the great hurts but from the little ones as well, and yet with whom she might fare onward, shoulder to shoulder, as God meant mates should fare.

"Surely 'tis not so unusual, this thing that I ask—only an honest man with human faults and human virtues, transfigured by a great love. And why is it that in this quest of mine, I have found him not?"

"Princess," said a voice at her doorway, "thou art surely still awake. The storm is lessening and there is naught to fear. I pray thee, try to sleep. And if there is aught I can do for thee, thou knowest thou hast only to speak."

From the warm darkness where she lay, Elaine saw his face with the firelight upon it, and all at once she knew.

"There is naught," she answered, with what he thought was coldness. "I bid thee leave me and take thine own rest."

"As thou wilt," he responded, submissively, but though the sound was now faint and far away, she still could hear him walking back and forth, keeping his unremitting guard.

So it was that at last Love came to the Lady Elaine. She had dreamed of some fair stranger, into whose eyes she should look and instantly know him for her lord, never guessing that her lord had gone with her when she left the Castle of Content. There was none of those leaps of the heart of which one of the maids at the Castle had read from the books while the others worked at the tapestry frames. It was nothing new, but only a light upon something which had always been, and which, because of her own blindness, she had not seen.

All through this foolish journey, Love had ridden beside the Lady Elaine, asking nothing but the privilege of serving her; demanding only the right to give, to sacrifice, to shield. And at last she knew.

135

*The doubting in her heart was for ever stilled and in its place was a great peace. There was an unspeakable tenderness and a measureless compassion, so wide and so deep that it sheltered all the world. For, strangely enough, the love of the many comes first through the love of the one.*

*The Lady Elaine did not need to ask whether he loved her, for, unerringly, she knew. Mated past all power of change, they two were one henceforward, though seas should roll between. Mated through suffering as well, for, in this new bond, as the Lady Elaine dimly perceived, there was great possibility of hurt. Yet there was no end or no beginning; it simply was, and at last she knew.*

*At length, she slept. When she awoke the morning was fair upon the mountains, but still he paced back and forth before her door. Rising, she bathed her face in the cool water he had brought her, braided her glorious golden hair, changed her soiled habit for a fresh robe of white satin traced with gold, donned her red embroidered slippers, and stepped out into the sunrise, shading her eyes with her hand until they grew accustomed to the dawn.*

*"Good morrow, Princess," he said. "We——"*

*Of a sudden, he stopped and fled like a wild thing into the forest, for by her eyes, he saw what was in her heart, and his hot words, struggling for utterance, choked him. "At last," he breathed, with his clenched hands on his breast; "at last—but no, 'tis another dream of mine that I dare not believe."*

*His senses reeled, for love comes not to a man as to a woman, but rather with the sound of trumpets and the glare of white light. The cloistered peace that fills her soul rests seldom upon him, and instead he is stirred with high ambition and spurred on to glorious achievement. For to her, love is the end of life; to him it is the means.*

*The knights thought it but another caprice when the Lady Elaine gave orders to return to the Castle of Content, at once, and by the shortest way—all save one of them. With his heart rioting madly through his breast, he knew, but he did not dare to look at Elaine. He was as one long blinded, who suddenly sees the sun.*

*So it was that though he still served her, he rode no longer by her side, and Elaine, hurt at first, at length understood, and smiled because of her understanding. All the way back, the Lady Elaine sang little songs to herself, and, the while she rode upon her palfrey, touched her zither into gentle harmonies. After many days, they came within sight of the Castle of Content.*

*As before, it was sunset, and the long light lay upon the hills, while the valley was in shadow. Purple were the vineyards, heavy with their clustered treasure, over which the tiny weavers had made their lace, and purple, too, were the many-spired cliffs, behind which the sunset shone.*

*A courier, riding swiftly in advance, had apprised the Lord of the Castle of Content of the return of the Lady Elaine, and the maids from the tapestry room, and the keeper of the wine-cellar, and the stable-boys, and the candle-makers, and the light-bearers all rushed out, heedless of their manners, for, one and all, they loved the Lady Elaine, and were eager to behold their beautiful mistress again.*

*But the Lord of the Castle of Content, speaking somewhat sternly, ordered them one and all back to their places, and, shamefacedly, they obeyed. "I would not be selfish," he muttered to himself, "but surely, Elaine is mine, and the first gleam of her beauty belongs of right to these misty old eyes of mine, that have long strained across the dark for the first hint of her coming. Of a truth her quest has been long."*

*So it came to pass that when the company reached the road that led down into the valley, the Lord of the Castle of Content was on the portico alone, though he could not have known that behind every shuttered window of the Castle, a humble servitor of Elaine's was waiting anxiously for her coming.*

*As before, Elaine rode at the head, waving her hand to her father, while the cymbals and the bugles crashed out a welcome. She could not see, but she guessed that he was there, and in return he waved a tremulous hand at her, though well he knew that in the fast gathering twilight, the child of his heart could not see the one who awaited her.*

*One by one, as they came in single file down the precipice, the old man counted them, much astonished to see that there was no new member of the company— that as many were coming back as had gone away. For the moment his heart was glad, then he reproached himself bitterly for his selfishness, and was truthfully most tender toward Elaine, because she had failed upon her quest.*

*The light gleamed capriciously upon the bauble of the fool, which he still carried, though now it hung downward from his saddle, foolishly enough. "A most merry fool," said the Lord of Content to himself. "I was wise to insist upon his accompanying this wayward child of mine."*

*Wayward she might be, yet her father's eyes were dim when she came down into the valley, where there was no light save the evening star, a taper light at an upper window of the Castle, and her illumined face.*

*"How hast thou fared upon thy quest, Elaine?" he asked in trembling tones, when at last she released herself from his eager embrace. He dreaded to hear her make known her disappointment, yet his sorrow was all for her, and not in the least for himself.*

*"I have found him, father," she said, the gladness in her voice betraying itself as surely as the music in a stream when Spring sets it free again, "and, forsooth, he rode with me all the time."*

*"Which knight hast thou chosen, Elaine?" he asked, a little sadly.*

*"No knight at all, dear father. I have found my knight in stranger guise than in armour and shield. He bears no lance, save for those who would injure me." And then, she beckoned to the fool.*

*"He is here, my father," she went on, her great love making her all unconscious of the shame she should feel.*

*"Elaine!" thundered her father, while the fool hung his head, "hast thou taken leave of thy senses? Of a truth, this is a sorry jest thou hast chosen to greet me with on thy return."*

*"Father," said Elaine, made bold by the silent pressure of the hand that secretly clasped hers, "'tis no jest. If thou art pained, indeed I am sorry, but if thou choosest to banish me, then this night will I go gladly with him I have chosen to be my lord. The true heart which Heaven has sent for me beats beneath his motley, and with him I must go. Dear father," cried Elaine, piteously, "do not send us away!"*

*The stern eyes of the Lord of the Castle of Content were fixed upon the fool, and in the gathering darkness they gleamed like live coals. "And thou," he said, scornfully; "what hast thou to say?"*

*"Only this," answered the fool; "that the Princess has spoken truly. We are mated by a higher law than that of thy land or mine, and 'tis this law that we must obey. If thou sayest the word, we will set forth to my country this very night, though we are both weary with much journeying."*

*"Thy land," said the Lord of the Castle, with measureless contempt, "and what land hast thou? Even the six feet of ground thou needest for a grave must be given thee at the last, unless, perchance, thou hast a handful of stolen earth hidden somewhere among thy other jewels!"*

*"Your lordship," cried the fool, with a clear ring in his voice, "thou shall not speak so to the man who is to wed thy daughter. I had not thought to tell even her till after the priests had made us one, but for our own protection, I am stung into speech.*

*"Know then, that I am no fool, but a Prince of the House of Bernard. My acres and my vineyards cover five times the space of this little realm of thine. Chests of gold and jewels I have, storehouses overflowing with grain and fine fabrics, three castles and a royal retinue. Of a truth, thou art blind since thou canst see naught but the raiment. May not a Prince wear motley if he chooses, thus to find a maid who will love him for himself alone?"*

*"Prince Bernard," muttered the Lord of Content, "the son of my old friend, whom I have long dreamed in secret shouldst wed my dear daughter Elaine! Your Highness, I beg you to forgive me, and to take my hand."*

*But Prince Bernard did not hear, nor see the outstretched hand, for Elaine was in his arms for the first time, her sweet lips close on his. "My Prince, oh my Prince," she murmured, when at length he set her free; "my eyes could not see, but my heart knew!"*

*So ended the Quest of the Lady Elaine.*

With a sigh, Harlan wrote the last words and pushed the paper from him, staring blankly at the wall and seeing nothing. His labour was at an end, all save the final copying, and the painstaking daily revision which would take weeks longer. The exaltation he had expected to be conscious of was utterly absent; instead of it, he had a sense of loss, of change.

His surroundings seemed hopelessly sordid and ugly, now that the glow was gone. All unknowingly, when Harlan pencilled: "The End," in fanciful letters at the bottom of the last page, he had had practically his last joy of his book. The torturing process of revision was to take all the life out of it. Sentences born of surging emotion would seem vapid and foolish when subjected to the cold, critical eye of his reason, yet he knew, dimly, that he must not change it too much.

"I'll let it get cool," he thought, "before I do anything more to it."

Yet, now, it was difficult to stop working. The rented typewriter, with its enticing bank of keys, was close at hand. A thousand sheets of paper and a box of carbon waited in the drawer of Uncle Ebeneezer's desk. His worn *Thesaurus of English Words and Phrases* was at his elbow. And they were poor. Then Harlan laughed, for they were no longer poor, and he had wholly forgotten it.

There was a step upon the porch outside, then Dorothy came into the hall. She paused outside the library door for a moment, ostensibly to tie her shoe, but in reality to listen. A wave of remorseful tenderness overwhelmed Harlan and he unlocked the door. "Come in," he said, smiling. "You needn't be afraid to come in any more. The book is all done."

"O Harlan, is it truly done?" There was no gladness in her voice, only relief. Doubt was in every intonation of her sentence; incredulity in every line of her body.

With this pitiless new insight of his, Harlan saw how she had felt for these last weeks and became very tenderly anxious not to hurt her; to shield his transformed self from her quick understanding.

"Really," he answered. "Have I been a beast, Dorothy?"

The question was so like the boy she used to know that her heart leaped wildly, then became portentously still.

"Rather," she admitted, grudgingly, from the shelter of his arms.

"I'm sorry. If you say so, I'll burn it. Nothing is coming between you and me." The words sounded hollow and meaningless, as he knew they were.

She put her hand over his mouth. "You won't do any such thing," she said. Dorothy had learned the bitterness of the woman's part, to stand by, utterly lonely, and dream, and wait, while men achieve.

"Can I read it now?" she asked, timidly.

"You couldn't make it out, Dorothy. When it's all done, and every word is just as I want it, I'll read it to you. That will be better, won't it?"

"Can Dick come, too?" She asked the question thoughtlessly, then flushed as Harlan took her face between his hands.

"Dorothy, did you know Dick before we were married?"

"Why, Harlan! I never saw him in all my life till the day he came here. Did you think I had?"

Harlan only grunted, but she understood, and, in return, asked her question. "Did you write the book about Elaine?" she began, half ashamed.

"Dear little idiot," said Harlan, softly. "I'd begun the book before she came or before I knew she was coming. I never saw her till she came to live with us. You're foolish, dearest, don't you think you are?"

He was swiftly perceiving the necessity of creating a new harmony to take the place of that old one, now so strangely lost.

"There are two of us," returned Dorothy, with conviction, wiping her eyes.

"I wish you'd ask me things," said Harlan, a little later. "I'm no mind reader. And, besides, the seventh son of a seventh son, born with a caul, and having three trances regularly every day after meals, never could hope to understand a woman unless she was willing to help him out a little, occasionally."

Which, after all, was more or less true.

# XVIII

## Uncle Ebeneezer's Diary

Harlan had taken his work upstairs, that the ceaseless clatter of the typewriter might not add to the confusion which normally prevailed in the Jack-o'-Lantern. Thus it happened that Dorothy was able to begin her long-cherished project of dusting, rearranging, and cataloguing the books.

There is a fine spiritual essence which exhales from the covers of a book. Shall one touch a copy of Shakespeare with other than reverent hands, or take up his Boswell without a smile? Through the worn covers and broken binding the master-spirit still speaks, no less than through the centuries which lie between. The man who had the wishing carpet, upon which he sat and wished and was thence immediately transported to the ends of the earth, was not possessed of a finer magic than one who takes his Boswell in his hands and then, for a golden quarter of an hour, lives in a bygone London with Doctor Johnson.

When the book-lover enters his library, no matter what storm and tumult may be in his heart, he has come to the inmost chamber of Peace. The indescribable, musty odour which breathes from the printed page is fragrant incense to him who loves his books. In unseemly caskets his treasures may be hidden, yet, when the cover is reverently lifted, the jewels shine with no fading light. The old, immortal beauty is still there, for any one who seeks it in the right way.

Dorothy had two willing assistants in Dick and Elaine. One morning, immediately after breakfast, the three went to the library and locked the door. Outside, the twins rioted unheeded and the perennially joyous Willie capered unceasingly. Mr. Perkins, gloomy and morose, wrote reams of poetry in his own room, distressed beyond measure by the rumble of the typewriter, but too much cast down to demand that it be stopped.

Mrs. Dodd and Mrs. Holmes, closely united through misfortune, were well-nigh inseparable now, while Mrs. Smithers, still sepulchral, sang continually in a loud, cracked voice, never by any chance happening upon the right note. As Dorothy said, when there are only eight tones in the octave, it would seem that sometime, somewhere, a warbler must coincide for a brief interval with the tune, but as Dick further commented, industry and patience can do wonders when rightly exercised.

Uncle Israel's midnight excursion to the orchard had given him a fresh attack of a familiar and distressing ailment to which he always alluded as "the brown kittys." Fortunately, however, the cure for asthma and bronchitis was contained in the same quart bottle, and needed only to be heated in order to work upon both diseases simultaneously.

Elaine rolled up the sleeves of her white shirt-waist, and turned in her collar, thereby producing an effect which Dick privately considered distractingly pretty. Dorothy was enveloped from head to foot in a voluminous blue gingham apron, and a dust cap, airily poised upon her smooth brown hair, completed a most becoming costume. Dick, having duly obtained permission, took off his coat and put on his hat, after which the library force was ready for action.

"First," said Dorothy, "we'll take down all the books." It sounded simple, but it took a good share of the day to do it, and the clouds of dust disturbed by the process produced sneezes which put Uncle Israel's feeble efforts to shame. When dusting the shelves, after they were empty, Elaine came upon a panel in the wall which slid back.

"Here's a secret drawer!" she cried, in wild delight. "How perfectly lovely! Do you suppose there's anything in it?"

Dorothy instantly thought of money and diamonds, but the concealed treasure proved to be merely a book. It was a respectable volume, however, at least as far as size was concerned, for Elaine and Dorothy together could scarcely lift it. It was a leather-bound ledger, of the most ponderous kind, and was fastened with a lock and key. The key, of course, was missing, but Dick soon pried open the fastening.

All but the last few pages in the book were covered with fine writing, in ink which was brown and faded, but still legible. It was Uncle Ebeneezer's penmanship throughout, except for a few entries at the beginning, in a fine, flowing feminine hand, which Dorothy instantly knew was Aunt Rebecca's.

"On the night of our wedding," the book began, "we begin this record of our lives, for until to-day we have not truly lived." This was signed by both. Then, in the woman's hand, was written a description of her wedding-gown, which was a simple white muslin, made by herself. Her ornaments were set down briefly—only a wreath of roses in her hair, a string of coral beads, and the diamond brooch which was at that moment in Dorothy's jewel-box.

For three weeks there were alternate entries, then suddenly, without date, were two words so badly written as to be scarcely readable: "She died." For days thereafter was only this: "I cannot write." These simple words were the key to a world of pain, for the pages were blistered with a man's hot tears.

142

Then came this: "She would want me to go on writing it, so I will, though I have no heart for it."

From thence onward the book proceeded without interruption, a minute and faithful record of the man's inner life. Long extracts copied from books filled page after page of this strange diary, interspersed with records of business transactions, of letters received and answered, of wages paid, and of the visits of Jeremiah Bradford.

"We talked long to-night upon the immortality of the soul," one entry ran. "Jeremiah does not believe it, but I must—or die."

Dick soon lost interest in the book, and finding solitary toil at the shelves uncongenial, went out, whistling. Elaine and Dorothy read on together, scarcely noting his absence.

The book had begun in the Spring. Early in June was chronicled the arrival of "a woman calling herself Cousin Elmira, blood relation of my Rebecca. Was not aware my Rebecca had a blood relation named Elmira, but there is much in the world that I do not know."

According to the diary, Cousin Elmira had remained six weeks and had greatly distressed her unwilling host. "Women are peculiar," Uncle Ebeneezer had written, "all being possessed of the devil, except my sainted Rebecca, who was an angel if there ever was one.

"Cousin Elmira is a curious woman. To-day she desired to know what had become of my Rebecca's wedding garments, her linen sheets and table-cloths. Answered that I did not know, and immediately put a lock upon the chest containing them. Have always been truthful up to now, but Rebecca would not desire to have any blood relation handling her sheets. Of this I am sure.

"Aug.. To-day came Cousin Silas Martin and his wife to spend their honeymoon. Much grieved to hear of Rebecca's death. Said she had invited them to spend their honeymoon with her when they married. Did not know of this, but our happiness was of such short duration that my Rebecca did not have time to tell me of all her wishes. Company is very hard to bear, but I would do much for my Rebecca.

"Aug. . This world can never be perfect under any circumstances, and trials are the common lot of humanity. We must all endeavour to bear up under affliction. Sarah Smithers is a good woman, most faithful, and does not talk a great deal, considering her sex. Not intending any reflection upon my Rebecca, whose sweet voice I could never hear too often.

"Aug. . Came Uncle Israel Skiles with a bad cough. Thinks the air of Judson Centre must be considered healthy as they are to build a sanitarium here. Did not know of the sanitarium.

"Aug. . Came Cousin Betsey Skiles to look after Uncle Israel. Uncle Israel not desiring to be looked after has produced some disturbance in my house.

"Aug. Cousin Betsey Skiles and Cousin Jane Wood, the latter arriving unexpectedly this morning, have fought, and Cousin Jane has gone away again. Had never met Cousin Jane Wood.

"Aug. . Was set upon by Cousin Silas Martin, demanding to know whether his wife was to be insulted by Cousin Betsey Skiles. Answered that I did not know.

"Aug. Was obliged to settle a dispute between Sarah Smithers and Cousin Betsey Skiles. Decided in favour of S. S., thereby angering B. S. Uncle Israel accidentally spilled his tonic on Cousin Betsey's clean apron. Much disturbance in my house.

"Aug. Cousin Silas Martin and wife went away, telling me they could no longer live with Cousin Betsey Skiles. B. S. is unpleasant, but has her virtues.

"Sept.. Uncle Israel thinks air of Judson Centre is now too chilly for his cough. Does not like his bed, considering it drafty. Says Sarah Smithers does not give him nourishing food.

"Sept.. Uncle Israel has gone.

"Sept. . Cousin Betsey Skiles has gone to continue looking after Uncle Israel. Sarah Smithers and myself now alone in peace.

All that Winter, the writing was of books, interspersed with occasional business details. In the Spring, the influx of blood relations began again and continued until Fall. The diary revealed the gradual transformation of a sunny disposition into a dark one, of a man with gregarious instincts into a wild beast asking only for solitude. Additions to the house were chronicled from time to time, with now and then a pathetic comment upon the futility of the additions.

Once there was this item: "Would go away for ever were it not that this was my Rebecca's home. Where we had hoped to be so happy, there is now a great emptiness and unnumbered Relations. How shall I endure Relations? Still they are all of her blood, though the most gentle blood does seem to take strange turns."

Again: "Do not think my Rebecca would desire to have all her kin visit her at once. Still, would do anything for my Rebecca. Have ordered five more beds."

As the years went by, the bitterness became more and more apparent. Long before the end, the record was frankly profane, and saddest of all was the evidence that under the stress of annoyance the great love for "my Rebecca" was slowly, but surely, becoming tainted. From simple profanity, Uncle Ebeneezer descended into blasphemous comment, modified at times by remorseful tenderness toward the dead.

"To-day," he wrote, "under pressure of my questioning, Sister-in-law Fanny Wood admitted that Rebecca had never invited her to come and see her. Asked Sister-in-law why she was here. Responded that Rebecca would have asked her if she had lived. Perhaps others have surmised the same. Fear of late I may have been unjust to my Rebecca."

Later on, "my Rebecca" was mentioned but rarely. She became "my dear companion," "my wife," or "my partner." The building of wings and the purchase of additional beds by this time had become a permanent feature, though, as the writer admitted, it was "a roundabout way."

"The easiest way would be to turn all out. Forgetting my duty to the memory of my dear companion, and sore pressed by many annoyances, did turn out Cousin Betsey Skiles, who forgave me for it without being so requested, and remained.

"Trains to Judson Centre," he wrote, at one time, "have been most grievously changed. One arrives just after breakfast, the other at three in the morning. Do not understand why this is, and anticipate new trouble from it."

The entries farther on were full of "trouble," being minute and intimate portrayals of the emotions of one roused from sleep at three in the morning to admit undesired guests, interlarded with pardonable profanity. "Seems that house might be altered in some way, but do not know. Will consult with Jeremiah."

After this came the record of an interview with the village carpenter, and rough sketches of proposed alterations. "Putting in new window in middle and making two upper windows round instead of square, with new porch-railing and two new narrow windows downstairs will do it. House fortunately planned by original architect for such alteration. Taking down curtains and keeping lights in windows nights should have some effect, though much doubt whether anything would affect Relations."

Soon afterward the oppressed one chronicled with great glee how a lone female, arriving on the night train, was found half-dead from fright by the roadside in the morning. "House *is* fearsome," wrote Uncle Ebeneezer, with evident relish. "Have been to Jeremiah's of an evening and, returning, found it wonderful to behold."

Presently, Dorothy came to an intimate analysis of some of the uninvited ones at present under her roof. The poet was given a full page of scathing comment, illustrated by rude caricatures, which were so suggestive that even Elaine thoroughly enjoyed them.

Pleased with his contribution to literature, Uncle Ebeneezer had written a long and keenly comprehensive essay upon each relation. These bits of vivid portraiture were numbered in this way: "Relation Number, Miss Betsey Skiles,

Claiming to be Cousin." At the end of this series was a very beautiful tribute to "My Dearly Beloved Nephew, James Harlan Carr, Who Has Never Come to See Me."

Frequently, thereafter, came pathetic references to "Dear Nephew James," "Unknown Recipient of an Old Man's Gratitude," "Discerning and Admirable James," and so on.

One entry ran as follows: "Have been approached this season by each Relation present in regard to disposal of my estate. Will fix surprise for all Relations before leaving to join my wife. Shall leave money to every one, though perhaps not as much as each expects. Jeremiah advises me to leave something to each. Laws are such, I believe, that no one remembered can claim more. Desire to be just, but strongly incline to dear Nephew James."

On the last page of all was a significant paragraph. "Dreamed of seeing my Rebecca once more, who told me we should be together again April 7th. Shall make all arrangements for leaving on that day, and prepare Surprises spoken of. Shall be very quiet in my grave with no Relations at hand, but should like to hear and see effect of Surprise. Jeremiah will attend."

The last lines were written on April sixth. "To-morrow I shall join my loved Rebecca and leave all Relations here to fight by themselves. Do not fear Death, but shudder at Relations. Relations keep life from being pleasant. Did not know my Rebecca was possessed of such numbers nor of such kinds, but forgive her all. Shall see her to-morrow."

Then, on the line below, in a hand that did not falter, was written: "The End."

Dorothy wiped her eyes on a corner of Elaine's apron, for Uncle Ebeneezer had been found dead in his bed on the morning of April seventh. "Elaine," she said, "what would you do?"

"Do?" repeated Elaine. "I'd strike one blow for poor old Uncle Ebeneezer! I'd order every single one of them out of the house to-morrow!"

"To-night!" cried Dorothy, fired with high resolve. "I'll do it this very night! Poor old Uncle Ebeneezer! Our sufferings have been nothing, compared to his."

"Are you going to tell Mr. Carr?" asked Elaine, wonderingly.

"Tell him nothing," rejoined Dorothy, with spirit. "He's got some old fogy notions about your house being a sacred spot where everybody in creation can impose on you if they want to, just because it is your house. I suppose he got it by being related to poor old uncle."

"Do I have to go, too?" queried Elaine, rubbing her soft cheek against Dorothy's.

"Not much," answered Mrs. Carr, with a sisterly embrace. "You'll stay, and Dick 'll stay, and that old tombstone in the kitchen will stay, and so will Claudius Tiberius, but the rest—MOVE!"

Consequently, Elaine looked forward to the dinner-hour with mixed anticipations. Mr. Perkins, Uncle Israel, Mrs. Dodd, and Mrs. Holmes each found a note under their plates when they sat down. Uncle Israel's face relaxed into an expression of childlike joy when he found the envelope addressed to him. "Valentine, I reckon," he said, "or mebbe it's sunthin' from Santa Claus."

"Queer acting for Santa Claus," snorted Mrs. Holmes, who had swiftly torn open her note. "Here we are, all ordered away from what's been our home for years, by some upstart relations who never saw poor, dear uncle. Are you going to keep boarders?" she asked, insolently, turning to Dorothy.

"No longer," returned that young woman, imperturbably. "I have done it just as long as I intend to."

Harlan was gazing curiously at Dorothy, but she avoided his eyes, and continued to eat as though nothing had happened. Dick, guessing rightly, choked, and had to be excused. Elaine's cheeks were flushed and her eyes sparkled, the flush deepening when Mrs.Dodd inquired where *her* valentine was. Mr. Perkins was openly dejected, and Mrs. Dodd, receiving no answer to her question, compressed her thin lips into a forced silence.

But Uncle Israel was moved to protesting speech. "'T is queer doin's for Santa Claus," he mumbled, pouring out a double dose of his nerve tonic. "'T ain't such a thing as he'd do, even if he was drunk. Turnin' a poor old man outdoor, what ain't got no place to go exceptin' to Betsey's, an' nobody can't live with Betsey. She's all the time mad at herself on account of bein' obliged to live with such a woman as she be. Summers I've allers stayed here an' never made no trouble. I've cooked my own food an' brought most of it, an' provided all my own medicines, an' even took my bed with me, goin' an' comin'. Ebeneezer's beds is all terrible drafty—I took two colds to once sleepin' in one of 'em—an' at my time of life 't ain't proper to change beds. Sleepin' in a drafty bed would undo all the good of bein' near the sanitarium. Most likely I'll have a fever or sunthin' now an' die."

"Shut up, Israel," said Mrs. Dodd, abruptly. "You ain't goin' to die. It wouldn't surprise me none if you had to be shot on the Day of Judgment before you could be resurrected. Folks past ninety-five that's pickled in patent medicine from the inside out, ain't goin' to die of no fever."

"Ninety-six, Belinda," said the old man, proudly. "I'll be ninety-six next week, an' I'm as young as I ever was."

"Then," rejoined Mrs. Dodd, tartly, "what you want to look out for is measles an' chicken-pox, to say nothin' of croup."

"Come, Gladys Gwendolen and Algernon Paul," interrupted Mrs. Holmes, in a high key; "we must go and pack now, to go away from dear uncle's. Dear uncle is dead, you know, and can't help his dear ones being ordered out of his house by upstarts."

"What's a upstart, ma?" inquired Willie.

"People who turn their dead uncle's relations out of his house in order to take boarders," returned Mrs. Holmes, clearly.

"Mis' Carr," said Mrs. Dodd, sliding up into Dick's vacant place, "have I understood that you want me to go away to-morrow?"

"Everybody is going away to-morrow," returned Dorothy, coldly.

"After all I've done for you?" persisted Mrs. Dodd.

"What have you done for me?" parried Dorothy, with a pleading look at Elaine.

"Kep' the others away," returned Mrs. Dodd, significantly.

"Uncle Ebeneezer does not want any of you here," said Dorothy, after a painful silence. The impression made by the diary was so vividly present with her that she felt as though she were delivering an actual message.

Much to her surprise, Mrs. Dodd paled and left the room hastily. Uncle Israel tottered after her, leaving his predigested food untouched on his plate and his imitation coffee steaming malodorously in his cup. Mr. Perkins bowed his head upon his hands for a moment; then, with a sigh, lightly dropped out of the open window. The name of Uncle Ebeneezer seemed to be one to conjure with.

"Dorothy," said Harlan, "might an obedient husband modestly inquire what you have done?"

"Elaine and I found Uncle Ebeneezer's diary to-day," explained Dorothy, "and the poor old soul was nagged all his life by relatives. So, in gratitude for what he's done for us, I've turned 'em out. I know he'd like to have me do it."

Harlan left his place and came to Dorothy, where, bending over her chair, he kissed her tenderly. "Good girl," he said, patting her shoulder. "Why in thunder didn't you do it months ago?"

"Isn't that just like a man?" asked Dorothy, gazing after his retreating figure.

"I don't know," answered Elaine, with a pretty blush, "but I guess it is."

# XIX

## Various Departures

"Algernon Paul," called Mrs. Holmes, shrilly, "let the kitty alone!"

Every one else on the premises heard the command, but "Algernon Paul," perhaps because he was not yet fully accustomed to his new name, continued forcing Claudius Tiberius to walk about on his fore feet, the rest of him being held uncomfortably in the air by the guiding influence.

"Algernon!" The voice was so close this time that the cat was freed by his persecutor's violent start. Seeing that it was only his mother, Algernon Paul attempted to recover his treasure again, and was badly scratched by that selfsame treasure. Whereupon Mrs. Holmes soundly cuffed Claudius Tiberius "for scratching dear little Ebbie, I mean Algernon Paul," and received a bite or two on her own account.

"Come, Ebbie, dear," she continued, "we are going now. We have been driven away from dear uncle's. Where is sister?"

"Sister" was discovered in the forbidden Paradise of the chicken-coop, and dragged out, howling. Willie, not desiring to leave "dear uncle's," was forcibly retrieved by Dick from the roof of the barn.

Mr. Harold Vernon Perkins had silently disappeared in the night, but no one feared foul play. "He'll be waitin' at the train, I reckon," said Mrs. Dodd, "an' most likely composin' a poem on 'Departure' or else breathin' into a tube to see if he's mad."

She had taken her dismissal very calmly after the first shock. "A woman what's been married seven times, same as I be," she explained to Dorothy, "gets used to bein' moved around from place to place. My sixth husband had the movin' habit terrible. No sooner would we get settled nice an' comfortable in a place, an' I got enough acquainted to borrow sugar an' tea an' molasses from my new neighbours, than Thomas would decide to move, an' more 'n likely, it'd be to some new town where there was a great openin' in some new business that he'd never tried his hand at yet. "My dear, I've been the wife of a undertaker, a livery-stable keeper, a patent medicine man, a grocer, a butcher, a farmer, an' a justice of the peace, all in one an' the same marriage. Seems 's if there wa'n't no business Thomas couldn't feel to turn his hand to, an' he knowed how they all ought to be run. If anybody was makin' a failure of anythin', Thomas

149

knowed just why it was failin' an' I must say he ought to know, too, for I never see no more steady failer than Thomas.

"They say a rollin' stone never gets no moss on it, but it gets worn terrible smooth, an' by the time I 'd moved to eight or ten different towns an' got as many as 'leven houses all fixed up, the corners was all broke off 'n me as well as off 'n the furniture. My third husband left me well provided with furniture, but when I went to my seventh altar, I didn't have nothin' left but a soap box an' half a red blanket, on account of havin' moved around so much.

"I got so's I'd never unpack all the things in any one place, but keep 'em in their dry-goods boxes an' barrels nice an' handy to go on again. When the movin' fit come on Thomas, I was always in such light marchin' order that I could go on a day's notice, an' that's the way we usually went. I told him once it'd be easier an' cheaper to fit up a prairie schooner such as they used to cross the plains in, an' then when we wanted to move, all we'd have to do would be to put a dipper of water on the fire an' tell the mules to get ap, but it riled him so terrible that I never said nothin' about it again, though all through my sixth marriage, it seemed a dretful likely notion.

"A woman with much marryin' experience soon learns not to rile a husband when 't ain't necessary. Sometimes I think the poor creeters has enough to contend with outside without bein' obliged to fight at home, though it does beat all, my dear, what a terrible exertion 't is for most men to earn a livin'. None of my husbands was ever obliged to fight at home an' I take great comfort thinkin' how peaceful they all was when they was livin' with me, an' how peaceful they all be now, though I think it's more 'n likely that Thomas is a-sufferin' because he can't move no more at present."

Her monologue was interrupted by the arrival of the stage, which Harlan had gladly ordered. Mrs. Holmes and the children climbed into it without vouchsafing a word to anybody, but Mrs. Dodd shook hands all around and would have kissed both Dorothy and Elaine had they not dodged the caress.

"Remember, my dear," said Mrs. Dodd to Dorothy; "I don't bear you no grudge, though I never was turned out of no place before. It's all in a lifetime, the same as marryin', and if I should ever marry again an' have a home of my own to invite you to, you an' your husband'll be welcome to come and stay with me as long as I've stayed with you, or longer, if you felt 'twas pleasant, an' I'd try to make it so."

The kindly speech made Dorothy very much ashamed of herself, though she did not know exactly why, and Gladys Gwendolen, with a cherubic smile, leaned out of the stage window and waved a chubby hand, saying: "Bye bye!"

Mrs. Holmes alone seemed hard and unforgiving, as she sat sternly upright, looking neither to the right nor the left.

"Rather unusual, isn't it?" whispered Elaine, as the ponderous vehicle turned into the yard, "to see so many of one's friends going on the stage at once?"

"Not at all," chuckled Dick. "Everybody goes on the stage when they leave the Carrs."

"Good bye, Belinda," yelled Uncle Israel, putting his flannel bandaged head out of one of the round upper windows. He had climbed up on a chair to do it. "I don't reckon I'll ever hear from you again exceptin' where Lazarus heard from the rich man!"

"Don't let that trouble you, Israel," shrieked Mrs. Dodd, piercingly. "I take it the rich man was diggin' for eight cents in Satan's orchard, an' didn't have no time to look up his friends."

The rejoinder seemed not to affect Uncle Israel, but it sent Dick into a spasm of merriment from which he recovered only when Harlan pounded him on the back.

"Come on," said Harlan, "it's not time to laugh yet. We've got to pack Uncle Israel's bed."

Uncle Israel was going on the afternoon train, and in another direction. He sat on his trunk and issued minute instructions, occasionally having the whole thing taken apart to be put together in a different kind of a parcel. As an especial favour, Dick was allowed to crate the bath cabinet, though as a rule, no profane hands were permitted to touch this instrument of health. Uncle Israel himself arranged his bottles, and boxes, and powders; a hand-satchel containing his medicines for the journey and the night.

"I reckon," he said, "if I take a double dose of my pain-killer, this noon, an' a double dose of my nerve tonic just before I get on the cars, I c'n get along with these few remedies till I get to Betsey's, where I'll have to take a full course of treatment to pay for all this travellin'. The pain-killer bottle an' the nerve tonic bottle is both dretful heavy, in spite of bein' only half full."

"How would it do," suggested Harlan, kindly, "to pour the nerve tonic into the pain-killer, and then you'd have only one bottle to carry. You mix them inside, anyway."

"You seem real intelligent, nephew," quavered Uncle Israel. "I never knowed I had no such smart relations. As you say, I mix 'em in my system anyway, an' it can't do no harm to do it in the bottle first."

No sooner said than done, but, strangely enough, the mixture turned a vivid emerald green, and had such a peculiarly vile odour that even Uncle Israel refused to have anything further to do with it.

"I shouldn't wonder but what you'd done me a real service, nephew," continued Uncle Israel. "Here I've been takin' this, month after month, an' never suspectin' what it was doin' in my insides. I've suspicioned for some time that the pain-killer wan't doin' me no good, an' I've been goin' to try Doctor Jones's Squaw Remedy, anyhow. I shouldn't wonder if my whole insides was green instead of red as they orter be. The next time I go to the City, I'm goin' to take this here compound to the healin' emporium where I bought it, an' ask 'em what there is in it that paints folk's insides. 'Tain't nothin' more 'n green paint."

The patient was so interested in this new development that he demanded a paint-brush and experimented on the porch railing, where it seemed, indeed, to be "green paint." In getting a nearer view, he touched his nose to it and acquired a bright green spot on the tip of that highly useful organ. Desiring to test it by every sense, he next put his ear down to the railing, as though he expected to hear the elements of the compound rushing together explosively.

"My hearin' is bad," he explained. "I wish you'd listen to this here a minute or two, nephew, an' see if you don't hear sunthin'." But Harlan, with his handkerchief pressed tightly to his nose, politely declined.

"I don't feel," continued Uncle Israel, tottering into the house, "as though a poor, sick man with green insides instead of red orter be turned out. Judson Centre is a terrible healthy place, or the sanitarium wouldn't have been built here, an' travellin' on the cars would shake me up considerable. I feel as though I was goin' to be took bad, an' as if I ought not to go. If somebody'll set up my bed, I'll just lay down on it an' die now. Ebeneezer would be willin' for me to die in his house, I know, for he's often said it'd be a reel pleasure to him to pay my funeral expenses if I c'd only make up my mind to claim 'em, an'," went on the old man pitifully, "I feel to claim 'em now. Set up my bed," he wheezed, "an' let me die. I'm bein' took bad."

He was swiftly reasoning himself into abject helplessness when Dick came valiantly to the rescue. "I'll tell you what, Uncle Israel," he said, "if you're going to be sick, and of course you know whether you are or not, we'll just get a carriage and take you over to the sanitarium. I'll pay your board there for a week, myself, and by that time we'll know just what's the matter with you."

The patient brightened amazingly at the mention of the sanitarium, and was more than willing to go. "I've took all kinds of treatment," he creaked, "but I ain't never been to no sanitarium, an' I misdoubt whether they've ever had anybody with green insides.

"I reckon," he added, proudly, "that that wanderin' pain in my spine'll stump 'em some to know what it is. Even in the big store where they keep all kinds of medicines, there couldn't nobody tell me. I know what disease 'tis, but I won't tell nobody. A man knows his own system best an' I reckon them smart doctors up at the sanitarium 'll be scratchin' their heads over such a complicated case as I be. Send my bed on to Betsey's but write on it that it ain't to be set up till I come. 'Twouldn't be worth while settin' it up at the sanitarium for a week, an' I'm minded to try a medical bed, anyways. I ain't never had none. Get the carriage, quick, for I feel an ailment comin' on me powerful hard every minute."

"Suppose," said Harlan, in a swift aside, "that they refuse to take the patient? What shall we do then?"

"We won't discuss that," answered Dick, in a low tone. "My plan is to leave the patient, drive away swiftly, and, an hour or so later, walk back and settle with the head of the repair shop for a week's mending in advance."

Harlan laughed gleefully, at which Uncle Israel pricked up his ears. "I'm in on the bill," he continued; "we'll go halves on the mending."

"Laughin'" said Uncle Israel, scornfully, "at your poor old uncle what ain't goin' to live much longer. If your insides was all turned green, you wouldn't be laughin'—you'd be thinkin' about your immortal souls."

It was late afternoon when the bed was finally dumped on the side track to await the arrival of the freight train, being securely covered with a canvas tarpaulin to keep it from the night dew and stray, malicious germs, seeking that which they might devour. Uncle Israel insisted upon overseeing this job himself, so that he did not reach the sanitarium until almost nightfall. Dick and Harlan were driving, and they shamelessly left the patient at the door of the Temple of Healing, with his crated bath cabinet, his few personal belongings, and his medicines.

Turning back at the foot of the hill, they saw that the wanderer had been taken in, though the bath cabinet still remained outside.

"Mean trick to play on a respectable institution," observed Dick, lashing the horses into a gallop, "but I'll go over in the morning and square it with 'em."

"I'll go with you," volunteered Harlan. "It's just as well to have two of us, for we won't be popular. The survivor can take back the farewell message to the wife and family of the other."

He meant it for a jest, but even in the gathering darkness, he could see the dull red mounting to Dick's temples. "I'll be darned," thought Harlan, seeing the whole situation instantly. Then, moved by a brotherly impulse, he said, cheerfully: "Go in and win, old man. Good luck to you!"

"Thanks," muttered Dick, huskily, "but it's no use. She won't look at me. She wants a nice lady-like poet, that's what she wants."

"No, she doesn't," returned Harlan, with deep conviction. "I don't claim to be a specialist, but when a man and a poet are entered for the matrimonial handicap, I'll put my money on the man, every time."

Dick swiftly changed the subject, and began to speculate on probable happenings at the sanitarium. They left the conveyance in the village, from whence it had been taken, and walked uphill.

Lights gleamed from every window of the Jack-o'-Lantern, but the eccentric face of the house had, for the first time, a friendly aspect. Warmth and cheer were in the blinking eyes and the grinning mouth, though, as Dick said, it seemed impossible that "no pumpkin seeds were left inside."

Those who do not believe in personal influence should go into a house which uninvited and undesired guests have regretfully left. Every alien element had gone from the house on the hill, yet the very walls were still vocal with discord. One expected, every moment, to hear Uncle Israel's wheeze, the shrill, spiteful comment of Mrs. Holmes, or a howl from one of the twins.

"What shall we do," asked Harlan, "to celebrate the day of emancipation?"

"I know," answered Dorothy, with a little laugh. "We'll burn a bed."

"Whose bed?" queried Dick.

"Mr. Perkins's bed," responded Elaine, readily. The tone of her voice sent a warm glow to Dick's heart, and he went to work at the heavy walnut structure with more gladness than exercise of that particular kind had ever given him before.

Harlan rummaged through the cellar and found a bottle of Uncle Ebeneezer's old port, which, for some occult reason, had hitherto escaped. Mrs. Smithers, moved to joyful song, did herself proud in the matter of fried chicken and flaky biscuit. Dorothy had taken all the leaves out of the table, so that now it was cosily set for four, and placed a battered old brass candlestick, with a tallow candle in it, in the centre.

"Seems like living, doesn't it?" asked Harlan. Until now, he had not known how surely though secretly distressed he had been by Aunt Rebecca's persistent kin. Claudius Tiberius apparently felt the prevailing cheerfulness, and purred vigorously, in Elaine's lap.

Afterward, they made a fire in the parlour, even though the night was so warm that they were obliged to have all the windows open, and, inspired by the portrait of Uncle Ebeneezer, discussed the peculiarities of his self-invited guests.

The sacrificial flame arising from the poet's bed directed the conversation to Mr. Perkins and his gift of song. Dick, though feeling more deeply upon the subject than any of the rest, was wise enough not to say too much.

"I found something under his mattress," remarked Dick, when the conversation flagged, "while I was taking his blooming crib apart to chop it up. I guess it must be a poem."

He drew a sorely flattened roll from his pocket, and slipped off the crumpled blue ribbon. It was, indeed, a poem, entitled "Farewell."

"I thought he might have been polite enough to say good bye," said Dorothy. "Perhaps it was easier to write it."

"Read it," cried Elaine, her eyes dancing. "Please do!"

So Dick read as follows:

All happy times must reach an end

Sometime, someday, somewhere,

A great soul seldom has a friend

Anyway or anywhere.

But one devoted to the Ideal

Must pass these things all by,

His eyes fixed ever on his Art,

Which lives, though he must die.

Amid the tide of cruel greed

Which laps upon our shore,

No one takes thought of the poet's need

Nor how his griefs may pour

Upon his poor, devoted head

And his sad, troubled heart;

But all these things each one must take,

Who gives his life to Art.

His crust of bread, his tick of straw

His enemies deny,

And at the last his patron saint

Will even pass him by;

The wide world is his resting place,

All o'er it he may roam,

And none will take the poet in,

Or offer him a home.

The tears of sorrow blind him now,

Misunderstood is he,

But thus great souls have always been,

And always they will be;

His eyes fixed ever on the Ideal

Will be there till he die,

To-night he goes, but leaves a poem

To say good bye, good bye!

"Poor Mr. Perkins," commented Dorothy, softly.

"Yes," mimicked Harlan, "poor Mr. Perkins. I don't see but what he'll have to work now, like any plain, ordinary mortal, with no 'gift'."

"What is the Ideal, anyway?" queried Elaine, looking thoughtfully into the embers of the poet's bedstead.

"That's easy," answered Dick, not without evident feeling. "It's whatever Mr. Perkins happens to be doing, or trying to do. He fixes it for the rest of us."

"I think," suggested Dorothy, after a momentary silence, "that the Ideal consists in minding your own business and gently, but firmly, assisting others to mind theirs."

All unknowingly, Dorothy had expressed the dominant idea of the dead master of the house. She fancied that the pictured face over the mantel was about to smile at her. Dorothy and Uncle Ebeneezer understood each other now, and she no longer wished to have the portrait moved.

Before they separated for the night, Dick told them all about the midnight gathering in the orchard, which he had witnessed from afar, and which the others enjoyed beyond his expectations.

"That's what uncle meant," said Elaine, "by 'fixing a surprise for relations.'" "I don't blame him," observed Harlan, "not a blooming bit. I wish the poor old duck could have been here to see it. Why wasn't I in on it?" he demanded of Dick, somewhat resentfully. "When anything like that was going on, why didn't you take me in?"

"It wasn't for me to interfere with his doings," protested Dick, "but I do wish you could have seen Uncle Israel."

At the recollection he went off into a spasm of merriment which bid fair to prove fatal. The rest laughed with him, not knowing just what it was about, such was the infectious quality of Dick's mirth.

"They've all gone," laughed Elaine, happily, taking her bedroom candle from Dorothy's hand, "they've all gone, every single one, and now we're going to have some good times."

Dick watched her as she went upstairs, the candlelight shining tenderly upon her sweet face, and thus betrayed himself to Dorothy, who had suspected for some time that he loved Elaine.

"Oh Lord!" grumbled Dick to himself, when he was safely in his own room. "Everybody knows it now, except her. I'll bet even Sis Smithers and the cat are dead next to me. I might as well tell her to-morrow as any time, the result will be just the same. Better do it and have it over with. The cat'll tell her if nobody else does."

But that night, strangely enough, Claudius Tiberius disappeared, to be seen or heard of no more.

# XX

## The Love of Another Elaine

When Dick and Harlan ventured up to the sanitarium, they were confronted by the astonishing fact that Uncle Israel was, indeed, ill. Later developements proved that he was in a measure personally responsible for his condition, since he had, surreptitiously, in the night, mixed two or three medicines of his own brewing with the liberal dose of a different drug which the night nurse gave him, in accordance with her instructions.

Far from being unconscious, however, Uncle Israel was even now raging violently against further restraint, and demanding to be sent home before he was "murdered."

"He's being killed with kindness," whispered Dick, "like the man who was run over by an ambulance."

Harlan arranged for Uncle Israel to stay until he was quite healed of this last complication, and then wrote out the address of Cousin Betsey Skiles, with which Dick was fortunately familiar. "And," added Dick, "if he's troublesome, crate him and send him by freight. We don't want to see him again."

Less than a week later, Uncle Israel and his bed were safely installed at Cousin Betsey's, and he was able to write twelve pages of foolscap, fully expressing his opinion of Harlan and Dick and the sanitarium staff, and Uncle Ebeneezer, and the rest of the world in general, conveying it by registered mail to "J. H. Car & Family." The composition revealed an astonishing command of English, particularly in the way of vituperation. Had Uncle Israel known more profanity, he undoubtedly would have incorporated it in the text.

"It reminds me," said Elaine, who was permitted to read it, "of a little coloured boy we used to know. A playmate quarrelled with him and began to call him names, using all the big words he had ever heard, regardless of their meaning. When his vocabulary was exhausted, our little friend asked, quietly: 'Is you froo?' 'Yes,' returned the other, 'I's froo.' 'Well then,' said the master of the situation, calmly, turning on his heel, 'all those things what you called me, you is.'"

"That's right," laughed Dick. "All those things Uncle Israel has called us, he is, but it makes him a pretty tough old customer."

A blessed peace had descended upon the house and its occupants. Harlan's work was swiftly nearing completion, and in another day or two, he would be ready to read the neatly typed pages to the members of his household. Dorothy could scarcely wait to hear it, and stole many a secret glance at the manuscript when Harlan was out of the house. Lover-like, she expected great things from it, and she saw the world of readers, literally, at her husband's feet. So great was her faith in him that she never for an instant suspected that there might possibly be difficulty at the start—that any publisher could be wary of this masterpiece by an unknown.

The Carrs had planned to remain where they were until the book was finished, then to take the precious manuscript, and go forth to conquer the City. Afterward, perhaps, a second honeymoon journey, for both were sorely in need of rest and recreation.

Elaine was going with them, and Dorothy was to interview the Personage whose private secretary she had once been, and see if that position or one fully as desirable could not be found for her friend. Also, Elaine was to make her home with the Carrs. "I won't let you live in a New York boarding house," said Dorothy warmly, "as long as we've any kind of a roof over our heads."

Dick had discovered that, as he expressed it, he must "quit fooling and get a job." Hitherto, Mr. Chester had preferred care-free idleness to any kind of toil, and a modest sum, carefully hoarded, represented to Dick only freedom to do as he pleased until it gave out. Then he began to consider work again, but as he seldom did the same kind of work twice, he was not particularly proficient in any one line.

Still, Dick had no false ideas about labour. At college he had canvassed for subscription books, solicited life and fire insurance, swept walks, shovelled snow, carried out ashes, and even handled trunks for the express company, all with the same cheerful equanimity. His small but certain income sufficed for his tuition and other necessary expenses, but for board at Uncle Ebeneezer's and a few small luxuries, he was obliged to work.

Just now, unwonted ambition fired his soul. "It's funny," he mused, "what's come over me. I never hankered to work, even in my wildest moments, and yet I pine for it this minute—even street-sweeping would be welcome, though that sort of thing isn't going to be much in my line from now on. With the start uncle's given me, I can surely get along all right, and, anyhow, I've got two hands, two feet, and one head, all good of their kind, so there's no call to worry."

Worrying had never been among Dick's accomplishments, but he was restless, and eager for something to do. He plunged into furniture-making with renewed energy, inspired by the presence of Elaine, who with her book or embroidery sat in her low rocker under the apple tree and watched him at his work.

Quite often she read aloud, sometimes a paragraph, now and then an entire chapter, to which Dick submitted pleasantly. He loved the smooth, soft cadence of Elaine's low voice, whether she read or spoke, so, in a way, it did not matter. But, one day, when she had read uninterruptedly for over an hour, Dick was seized with a violent fit of coughing.

"I say," he began, when the paroxysm had ceased; "you like books, don't you?"

"Indeed I do—don't you?"

"Er—yes, of course, but say—aren't you tired of reading?"

"Not at all. You needn't worry about me. When I'm tired, I'll stop."

She was pleased with his kindly thought for her comfort, and thereafter read a great deal by way of reward. As for Dick, he burned the midnight candle over many a book which he found inexpressibly dull, and skilfully led the conversation to it the next day. Soon, even Harlan was impressed by his wide knowledge of literature, though no one noted that about books not in Uncle Ebeneezer's library, Dick knew nothing at all.

Dorothy spent much of her time in her own room, thus forcing Dick and Elaine to depend upon each other for society. Quite often she was lonely, and longed for their cheery chatter, but sternly reminded herself that she was being sacrificed in a good cause. She built many an air castle for them as well as for herself, furnishing both, impartially, with Elaine's old mahogany and the simple furniture Dick was making out of Uncle Ebeneezer's relics.

By this time the Jack-o'-Lantern was nearly stripped of everything which might prove useful, and they were burning the rest of it in the fireplace at night. "Varnished hardwood," as Dick said, "makes a peach of a blaze."

Meanwhile Harlan was labouring steadfastly at his manuscript. The glowing fancy from which the book had sprung was quite gone. Still, as he cut, rearranged, changed, interlined, reconstructed and polished, he was not wholly unsatisfied with his work. "It may not be very good," he said to himself, "but it's the best I can do—now. The next will be better, I'm sure." He knew, even then, that there would be a "next one," for the eternal thirst which knows no quenching had seized upon his inmost soul.

Hereafter, by an inexplicably swift reversion, he should see all life as literature, and literature as life. Friends and acquaintances should all be, in his inmost consciousness, ephemeral. And Dorothy—dearly as he loved her, was separated from him as by a veil.

Still, as he worked, he came gradually to a better adjustment, and was very tenderly anxious that Dorothy should see no change in him. He had not yet reached the point, however, where he would give it all up for the sake of finding things real again, if only for an hour.

Day after day, his work went on. Sometimes he would spend an hour searching for a single word, rightly to express his meaning. Page after page was re-copied upon the typewriter, for, with the nice conscience of a good workman, Harlan desired a perfect manuscript, at least in mechanical details.

Finally, he came to the last page and printed "The End" in capitals with deep satisfaction. "When it's sandpapered," he said to himself, "and the dust blown off, I suppose it will be done."

The "sandpapering" took a week longer. At the end of that time, Harlan concluded that any manuscript was done when the writer had read it carefully a dozen times without making a single change in it. On a Saturday night, just as the hall clock was booming eleven, he pushed it aside, and sat staring blankly at the wall for a long time.

"I don't know what I've got," he thought, "but I've certainly got two hundred and fifty pages of typed manuscript. It should be good for something—even at space rates."

After dinner, Sunday, he told them that the book was ready, and they all went out into the orchard. Dick was resigned, Elaine pleasantly excited, Dorothy eager and aflame with triumphant pride, Harlan self-conscious, and, in a way, ashamed.

As he read, however, he forgot everything else. The mere sound of the words came with caressing music to his ears. At times his voice wavered and his hands trembled, but he kept on, until it grew so dark that he could no longer see.

They went into the house silently, and Dick touched a match to the fire already laid in the fireplace, while Dorothy lighted the candles and the reading lamp. The afterglow faded and the moon rose, yet still they rode with Elaine and her company, through mountain passes and over blossoming fields, past many dangers and strange happenings, and ever away from the Castle of Content.

Harlan's deep, vibrant voice, now stern, now tender, gave new meaning to his work. His secret belief in it gave it a beauty which no one else would ever see. Dorothy, listening so intently that it was almost pain, never took her eyes from his face. In that hour, if Harlan could have known it, her woman's soul was kneeling before his, naked and unashamed.

Dick privately considered the whole thing more or less of a nuisance, but the candlelight touched Elaine's golden hair lovingly, and the glow from the fire seemed to rest caressingly upon her face. All along, he saw a clear resemblance between his Elaine and the lady of the book, also, more keenly, a closer likeness between himself and the fool who rode at her side.

When Harlan came to the song which the fool had written, and which he had so shamelessly revised and read aloud at the table, Dick seriously considered a private and permanent departure, like the nocturnal vanishing of Mr. Perkins, without even a poem for farewell.

Elaine, lost in the story, was heedless of her surroundings. It was only at the last chapter that she became conscious of self at all. Then, suddenly, in her turn, she perceived a parallel, and quivered painfully with a new emotion.

*"Some one, perchance," mused the Lady Elaine, "whose beauty my eyes alone should perceive, whose valour only I should guess before there was need to test it. Some one great of heart and clean of mind, in whose eyes there should never be that which makes a woman ashamed. Some one fine-fibred and strong-souled, not above tenderness when a maid was tired. One who should make a shield of his love, to keep her not only from the great hurts but from the little ones as well, and yet with whom she might fare onward, shoulder to shoulder, as God meant mates should fare."*

Like the other Elaine, she saw who had served her secretly, asking for no recognition; who had always kept watch over her so unobtrusively and quietly that she never guessed it till now. Like many another woman, Elaine had dreamed of her Prince as a paragon of beauty and perfection, with unconscious vanity deeming such an one her true mate. Now her story-book lover had gone for ever, and in his place was Dick; sunny-hearted, mischievous, whistling, clear-eyed Dick, who had laughed and joked with her all Summer, and now— must never know.

In a fierce agony of shame, she wondered if he had already guessed her secret—if she had betrayed it to him before she was conscious of it herself; if that was why he had been so kind. Harlan was reading the last page, and Elaine shaded her face with her hand, determined, at all costs, to avoid Dick, and to go away to-morrow, somewhere, anywhere.

*But Prince Bernard did not hear*, read Harlan, *nor see the outstretched hand, for Elaine was in his arms for the first time, her sweet lips close on his. "My Prince, Oh, my Prince," she murmured, when at length he set her free; "my eyes did not see but my heart knew!"*

*So ended the Quest of the Lady Elaine.*

The last page of the manuscript fluttered, face downward, upon the table, and Dorothy wiped her eyes. Elaine's mouth was parched, but she staggered to her feet, knowing that she must say some conventional words of congratulation to Harlan, then go to her own room.

Blindly, she put out her hand, trying to speak; then, for a single illuminating instant, her eyes looked into Dick's.

With a little cry, Elaine fled from the room, overwhelmed with shame. In a twinkling, she was out of the house, and flying toward the orchard as fast as her light feet would carry her, her heart beating wildly in her breast.

By the sure instinct of a lover, Dick knew that his hour had come. He dropped out of the window and overtook her just as she reached her little rocking-chair, which, damp with the Autumn dew, was still under the apple tree.

"Elaine!" cried Dick, crushing her into his arms, all the joy of youth and love in his voice. "Elaine! My Elaine!"

"The audience," remarked Harlan, in an unnatural tone, "appears to have gone. Only my faithful wife stands by me."

"Oh, Harlan," answered Dorothy, with a swift rush of feeling, "you'll never know till your dying day how proud and happy I am. It's the very beautifullest book that anybody ever wrote, and I'm so glad! Mrs. Shakespeare could never have been half as pleased as I am! I——," but the rest was lost, for Dorothy was in his arms, crying her heart out for sheer joy.

"There, there," said Harlan, patting her shoulders awkwardly, and rubbing his rough cheek against her tear-wet face; "it wasn't meant to make anybody cry."

"Why can't I cry if I want to?" demanded Dorothy, resentfully, between sobs.

Harlan's voice was far from even and his own eyes were misty as he answered: "Because you are my own darling girl and I love you, that's why."

They sat hand in hand for a long time, looking into the embers of the dying fire, in the depths of that wedded silence which has no need of words. The portraits of Uncle Ebeneezer and Aunt Rebecca seemed fully in accord, and, though mute, eloquent with understanding.

"He'd be so proud," whispered Dorothy, looking up at the stern face over the mantel, "if he knew what you had done here in his house. He loved books, and now, because of his kindness, you can always write them. You'll never have to go back on the paper again."

Harlan smiled reminiscently, for the hurrying, ceaseless grind of the newspaper office was, indeed, a thing of the past. The dim, quiet room was his, not the battle-ground of the street. Still, as he knew, the smell of printer's ink in his nostrils would be like the sound of a bugle to an old cavalry horse, and even now, he would not quite trust himself to walk down Newspaper Row.

"I love Uncle Ebeneezer and Aunt Rebecca," went on Dorothy, happily. "I love everybody. I've love enough to-night to spare some for the whole world."

"Dear little saint," said Harlan, softly, "I believe you have."

The clock struck ten and the fire died down. A candle flickered in its socket, then went out. The chill Autumn mist was rising, and through it the new moon gleamed faintly, like veiled pearl.

"I wonder," said Harlan, "where the rest of the audience is? If everybody who reads the book is going to disappear suddenly and mysteriously, I won't be the popular author that I pine to be."

"Hush," responded Dorothy; "I think they are coming now. I'll go and let them in."

Only a single candle was burning in the hall, and when Dorothy opened the door, it went out suddenly, but in that brief instant, she had seen their glorified faces and understood it all. The library door was open, and the dimly lighted room seemed like a haven of refuge to Elaine, radiantly self-conscious, and blushing with sweet shame.

"Hello," said Dick, awkwardly, with a tremendous effort to appear natural, "we've just been out to get a breath of fresh air."

It had taken them two hours, but Dorothy was too wise to say anything. She only laughed—a happy, tender, musical little laugh. Then she impulsively kissed them both, pushed Elaine gently into the library, and went back into the parlour to tell Harlan.

# The End